CONTENTS

INTRODUCTION

Macramé is a craft based on knotting. The technique has been used for making accessories for hundreds of years; in the 19th century it was used to decorate household linen and shawls. In the 1970s and 80s it became one of the most popular creative arts.

For many people, macramé is associated with hippy-style plant holders, but there is much more to this technique. Nowadays, it is a common feature of South American craftwork, particularly in jewellery and accessories. Different generations have embraced the fashion for macramé without even knowing it; they refer to their knotting projects by other names, such as scoubidous, friendship bracelets and shamballa jewellery. In recent times, it has been a big trend in American and Australian home interiors.

Macramé is easy to learn and does not require a huge quantity of materials. Once you have mastered the main knots, it is a simple matter of combining them to create flat strips or 3-D objects. In terms of basic materials, anything goes as long as the yarn is sufficiently strong and flexible. Feel free to play around with diameters, materials, number of threads, combinations of lines, colours and knots: the results are endless.

MATERIALS

There are materials specifically marketed for macramé, but with a bit of imagination you can easily manage without.

A KNOTTING BOARD

You can buy foam knotting boards. They come in various formats but are divided into squares so you can keep track of the measurements of your work. Notches on the edges hold your threads in place. Search 'macramé board' to find them on the Internet. Failing this you can use a piece of cork board glued onto wood to make it rigid or, more simply still, some very thick cardboard. A clipboard with a metal clip at the top is ideal for macramé jewellery-making.

ESSENTIAL TOOLS

▶ Pins, macramé pins
Essential for holding your work in place on the macramé board. Specific macramé pins are ideal; they are T-shaped and quite thick. Otherwise, dressmaker's pins will do.

▶ A metal bulldog clip
In some cases, when the yarn is too thick, too fine or very fragile a clip works better than pins. The clip itself can be pinned onto your board.

▶ A pair of scissors
▶ A tape measure
▶ Adhesive tape
Used for wrapping around the ends of the yarn. Tape allows you to identify different strands, prevents the yarn from fraying and helps when threading yarn through beads. Masking tape is better than ordinary adhesive tape as it does not pull the yarn apart.

FOR FINISHING

▶ Jewellery pliers
Used for opening and closing findings and clasps.

▶ A yarn needle with a large eye
To thread the yarn through to the back of the finished work.

▶ A medium-sized crochet hook
To pull the yarn through knots.

▶ Fabric glue or hot-melt glue gun
Used for fixing knots firmly and preventing yarn from fraying. Fabric glue is used for fine yarn and the hot-melt glue gun for yarns of more than 2mm (1/16in) diameter. Hot-melt glue is also used for some findings and clasps.

THE YARN

In principle, as long as the yarn is strong and flexible, it can be knotted. In this book we have stuck to using the main types of yarn.

▶ Cabled cotton twine
This most traditional macramé yarn is composed of several entwined strands. It is easily available in 20m (22yd) balls from hardware shops and usually comes in several diameters (from 1.5mm/1/16in to 7mm/1/4in and more). Cotton twine or string normally comes in its natural colour which makes it easy to dye.

▶ Cotton cord
Cotton cord comes in 1 or 2mm (1/25 or 1/16in) diameter and a wide variety of colours. It is particularly used for micro-macramé and jewellery.

▶ **Crochet cotton**
A very fine cotton twine, 5 to 8mm (¼ to ⅜in) diameter. Available from haberdashery stores.

▶ **Natural twine and string, made from hemp, jute, sisal, linen or coconut**
These are gardening twines, available in a 2mm (¹⁄₁₆in) diameter. Their natural colours make them an attractive material to use for many projects. Jute and hemp are also often available in several different colours.

▶ **Embroidery yarn, pearl cotton**
Used for micro-macramé jewellery. Great for the range of colours on offer.

▶ **Waxed cotton, shiny or matt**
Stiffer than embroidery yarn or cotton twine. Comes in a 1 or 2mm (¹⁄₂₅ or ¹⁄₁₆in) diameter and a wide range of colours. Ideal for jewellery and small accessories.

▶ **Jersey yarn or Hoooked Zpagetti**
Slightly elastic cotton jersey yarn (T-shirt material). It is quite broad, between 1 and 2cm (½ to ¾in). It is a very nice to work with, particularly for accessories and fashion items. There is a range of printed varieties for more unusual designs.

▶ **Leather laces, suede and knitting leather**

▶ **Round or flat cords**
Knotted or braided for accessories.

▶ **Wool**
Wool can be used , but it is often not stiff enough and comes apart when handled.

▶ **Scoubidou laces**
Only available in 50cm (19¾in) or 1m (1yd) lengths which limits their use.

HINTS & TIPS

DIMENSIONS AND LENGTH OF YARN

▶ The size of the finished work and the amount of yarn required depends on the diameter of the yarn used, the tension of your knots and the space between them. For macramé you should generally use lengths of yarn 4 to 7 times longer than the final product.

▶ It is worth making a sample before starting work on a new piece. Measure the length of the yarn before starting and knot it over a few centimetres. Calculate the length of yarn remaining in relation to how much you started with.

▶ Always cut yarn a little too long.

IDENTIFYING THE THREADS

▶ In order to avoid getting the different strands mixed up, or so you can number them, you might like to mark some specific, important strands. This can be done by wrapping coloured adhesive tape around the ends.

▶ Make sure knots are formed properly before pulling them tight.

GLOSSARY

▶ **Yarn:** This generic term is used before the project begins.

▶ **Lengths:** Refers to the cut yarn.

▶ **Threads:** Refers to the pieces when they are set onto the 'holding cord' on your work board.

▶ **Leader cord:** The majority of knots require several threads to be worked. Some of these may be 'dormant' and are only used to hold the 'working threads'. The leader cord will be the same length as the final length of the series of knots. You can use as many leader cords as you like. The more leader cords there are, the bigger the knots.

▶ **Working thread:** This is the thread that is worked around the leader cord. It will measure 3 to 7 times the final length of the series of knots.

▶ **Holding cord:** Fixed thread onto which the lengths of yarn will be 'set on'.

▶ **Braid:** A braid is formed by a series of vertical knots, for example a plait.

▶ **Panel:** Panels are created using a series of knots running across horizontal rows. Adding further rows creates a solid panel, like knitting.

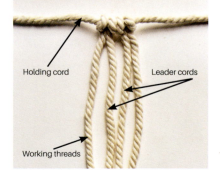

Holding cord

Leader cords

Working threads

TECHNIQUE 1

PRACTICAL KNOTS

The coil knot, overhand knot and collecting knot are all you need to get started on a braided design.

OVERHAND KNOT

The overhand knot allows you to tie several lengths together in the simplest way possible. This knot can be done using all the lengths. The more lengths you use, the bigger the knot.

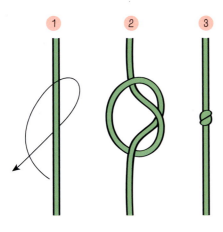

OVERHAND KNOT USING SEVERAL THREADS

COLLECTING KNOT

The collecting knot is a variation on the overhand knot.

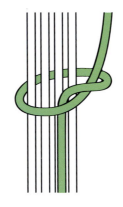

COIL KNOT

The coil knot allows you to hold all the threads together with another thread, particularly at the ends. Bring a separate thread across the top of the threads that have been gathered together. Form a loop and then wind the thread tightly around the loop and the bundle of threads. Ensure as you wind that the coils of thread are next to each other, not on top of each other. Continue winding until you reach the desired length (1). Pass the end through the loop. Draw both ends gently in opposite directions. The loop then disappears under the coils and is locked into place (2). Trim off the ends (3).

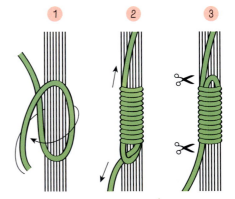

STARTING YOUR MACRAMÉ

There are several ways of starting a piece of macramé. The technique you choose will depend on the effect you want to achieve and the number of lengths you are using.

TYING TOGETHER AND WORKING THE FREE LENGTHS

Align the lengths, then knot them together using an overhand knot or collecting knot. This may or may not be a temporary knot, but serves as a starting point for the next series of knots.

MAKING A LOOP

This is often used as a starting point, as it allows you to make an attachment.

• Line up the pieces and fold them in half. ▼

Middle of the lengths

You then have several options:

• Knot all the threads together using an overhand knot under the loop. ▼

• Knot a single thread around the others and start a series of knots, ensuring that the length of the loop remains free. ▼

Working thread

Leader cord

• Tie a collecting knot. ▼

• The plaited loop (see also Technique 2, page 22). Make a temporary overhand knot at the start of the loop, but do not pull it too tight. Braid a 3-ply plait to the required length. ▼

When you have finished plaiting, undo the temporary knot. Knot a new thread at the start of the plait to close the loop. ▼

WORKING IN SYMMETRY

This method allows you to work on either side of a bead. Tie an overhand knot using all the lengths at the position where the bead will be located. Thread on the bead and braid a plait. Undo the temporary knot and plait in the opposite direction. ▼

2nd plait from right to left ←   → 1st plait from left to right

PINK BRACELET

An easy-to-make bracelet that is a good introduction to braiding. The coil knot is a technical knot that is also very decorative.

YOU WILL NEED

▶ 270cm (106½in) cabled cotton twine, 2.5mm (⁹⁄₁₀in) diameter
▶ One DMC embroidery yarn art. 117 no. 4200
▶ Hot-melt glue gun

STEP BY STEP

1. Cut 3 pieces of cabled cotton twine, 90cm (35½in) in length. Align them and tie a temporary overhand knot 2cm (¾in) from the end using all the lengths.

2. Cut 12 pieces of embroidery yarn, 60cm (23½in) in length. Work coil knots along each length of the cotton yarn, creating a 6cm (2½) loop for each coil knot. One 60cm (23½) length will give you a 4cm (1½in) coil knot.

3. A coil knot should always overlap the last two coils of the previous coil knot.

2 cm (¾in)

Loop of the coil knot: 6cm (2½in)

4. Once the embroidery yarn covers 15cm (6in) of all 3 cotton cords, plait a tight braid with the 3 strands of the uncovered cotton twine.

TO FINISH

5-6. Form a loop with the braid and stick the threads together using the hot-melt glue gun. Tie a final coil knot over the glued area using 40cm (15¾in) of embroidery yarn.

7. Undo the first temporary knot and plait the 3 threads loosely. Align with the excess threads of the first 3 coil knots. Tie another overhand knot, pulling it tight to form a 'button' to go through the 'buttonhole' at the other end. Trim all the threads to the required length.

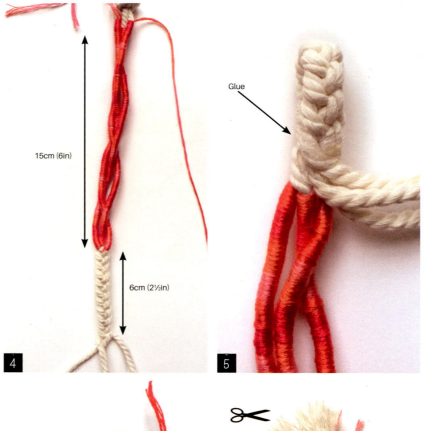

15cm (6in)

6cm (2½in)

4

Glue

5

6

7

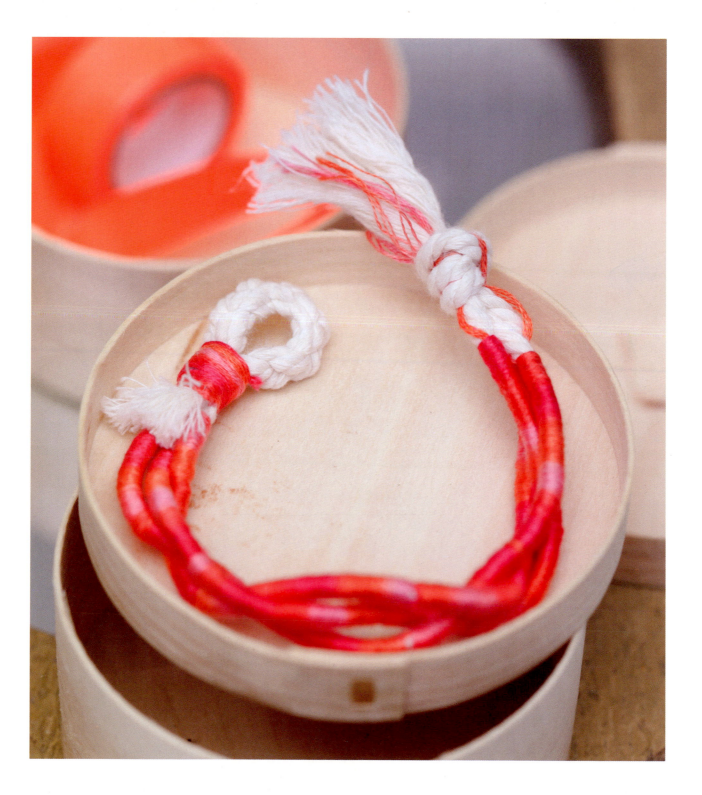

RAINBOW NECKLACE

A long necklace made with coil knots of coloured yarn and copper wire.

YOU WILL NEED

- 4.5m (5yd) cabled cotton twine, 2.5mm (¹⁄₁₆in) diameter
- One DMC embroidery yarn no. 966, 907, 93, 349, 307, 51, 947; two no. 959 and 893 (coil knots for finishing)
- 10 wooden beads of various sizes and colours
- A 6m (6½yd) spool of 2mm (¹⁄₁₆in) copper wire
- Jewellery wire cutters

STEP BY STEP

1-2. Cut 5 pieces of cabled cotton twine, 85cm (33½in) in length. Wrap adhesive tape round the ends so they do not fray. From the embroidery yarn, cut four 2m (2⅛yd) lengths of no. 893 and four 2m (2⅛yd) lengths of no. 959 for the final coil knot. Cut the rest of the embroidery yarn into 60cm (23½in) lengths. Each length allows for a 5cm (2in) coil knot with a 7cm (2¾in) loop underneath.

Tie coil knots for 77cm (30¼in), varying the colours.

3. To strengthen the coil knots, wind the first few coils of each knot over the last one.

7cm (2¾in) loop

TO FINISH

4. Wrap a piece of adhesive tape round the ends of the 5 threads.

5. Align two 2m (2⅛yd) lengths of no. 959 and two 2m (2⅛yd) lengths of no. 893 and use them to work a 4cm (1½in) coil knot.

6. At both ends of the necklace, thread on a bead. Thread the strands through the hole in the bead twice to hold it firmly in place and tie an overhand knot through all the strands.

7. Use the remaining lengths to braid a 45cm (17¾in) 3-ply plait (1 pink strand – 2 green strands – 1 pink strand). Tie all the strands together in an overhand knot. Thread a bead onto each strand of the plait and hold it in place with an overhand knot.

8-9. Cut some 20cm (7¾in) pieces of copper wire and coil them tightly around the necklace.

4

5

7

8

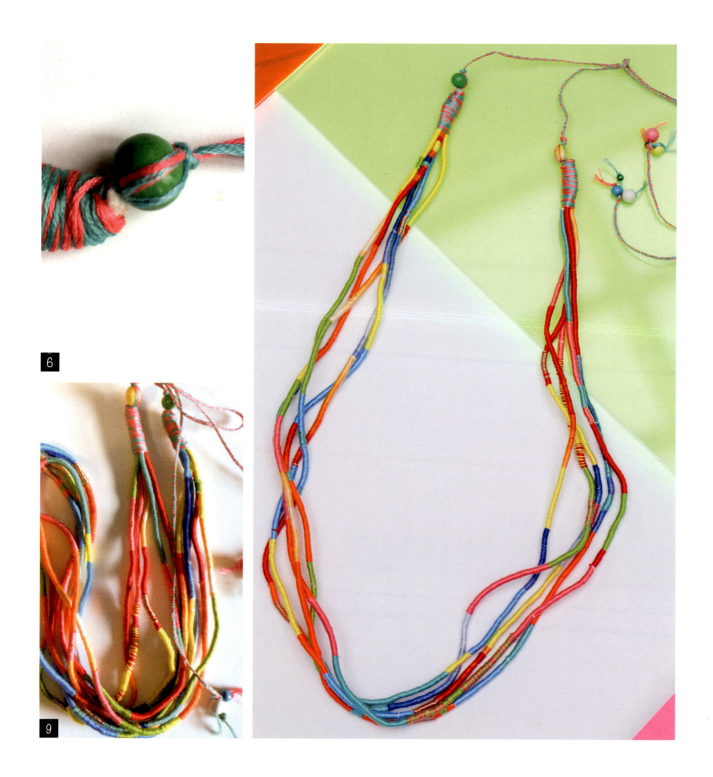

6

9

BLACK MESH CUFF

Overhand knots, technical and super-simple knots form a mesh when they are arranged in an alternating pattern. This small piece of mesh-work creates a striking cuff bracelet.

YOU WILL NEED
For a 15cm (6in) cuff (not including clasp)

▶ 7.5m (8yd) of DMC embroidery yarn, art. 89
  no. 2310
▶ 1 wooden bead, 8mm (⅜in) diameter

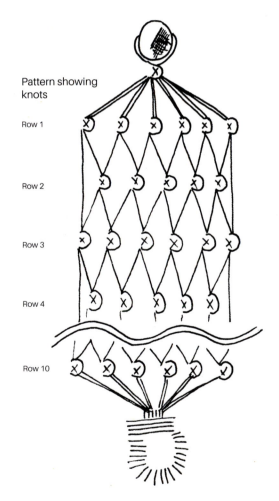

Pattern showing knots

Row 1

Row 2

Row 3

Row 4

Row 10

STEP BY STEP

1-A. Cut six 90cm (35½in) lengths of embroidery yarn. Slide the bead to the middle of one of the lengths. Bring the two halves of the thread down around the bead and tie them into an overhand knot.

2. Fold the 5 remaining lengths in half and place them beneath the threads under the bead.

3. Tie all the strands together in an overhand knot. Divide the threads into 6 groups of 2 threads each.

4. Row 1: 1cm (½in) from the knot, tie an overhand knot in each group of 2 threads.

5. Row 2: leaving the first and the last thread unworked, tie an overhand knot in the next 2 threads, alternating with the previous ones.

6. Continue to alternate in this way until row 10, following the pattern.

TO FINISH

7-8-9. At the end of 10 rows, 2cm (¾in) from the last knots, use one of the threads to tie a collecting knot around all the others. Cut a 1.2m (1.3yd) length of yarn and work a 4cm (1½in) coil knot, forming a loop (**B**). Work another coil knot around all the strands to hold the loop securely in place. Trim off the ends.

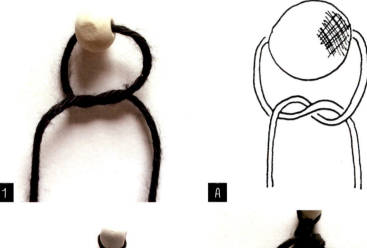

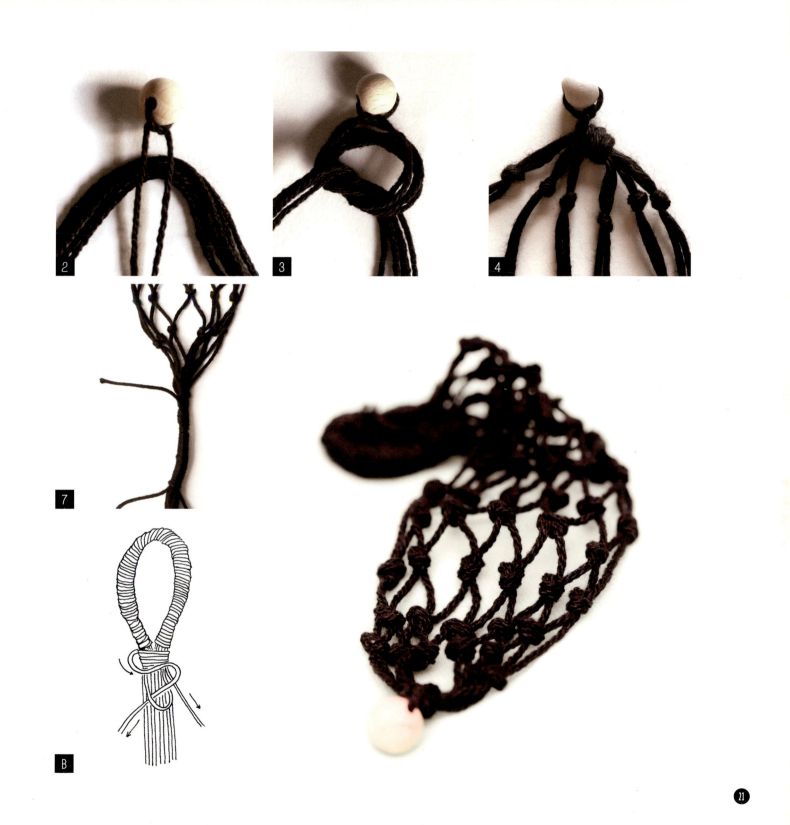

TECHNIQUE 2

PLAITS AND BRAIDS

Everyone knows how to braid a plait. The more threads you use, the thicker and more attractive the plait. Plaiting is used to make pretty scoubidou bracelets.

3-PLY PLAIT

This is the most commonly used plait.

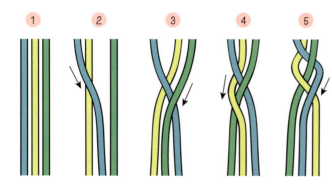

5-PLY PLAIT

A very commonly used plait. Cross the 2 outside threads (2-3), then plait the 3 remaining strands in order (4-5-6). Repeat stages 2 to 6. Pull tight as you plait (4-5-6).

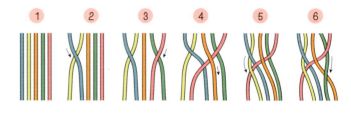

4-PLY PLAIT

Cross the threads in the order shown in the diagrams.

4-PLY ROUND BRAID

A round braid using 4 threads tied together with an overhand knot at one end or with 2 threads laid out in a cross shape.

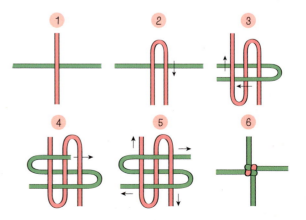

TECHNIQUE 3

FLAT KNOT

The flat knot is the most widely used in macramé. Depending on the diameter of the yarn used and the distance between the knots, the results can be very different.

FLAT KNOT

The flat knot is one of the most commonly used knots for jewellery, accessories and decoration. It is the basis for numerous combinations of braids or panels. It is a knot formed in 2 parts, or by 2 half-knots. It generally uses 4 lengths: 2 leader threads in the centre and 2 working threads on either side. The leader cords will be the same length as the completed project while the working threads need to be 5 to 7 times longer. By increasing the number of leader threads, you increase the width of the flat knot. Pull each knot equally tight.

PEA KNOT

The pea knot is a bulkier version of the flat knot. For each pea, work 3 flat knots (1). Bring the 2 leader cords up and through the spaces between the 2 outside threads to turn the braid in on itself (2). Bring the 2 threads down underneath the knot you have formed and draw downwards to form the pea (3). Work a flat knot just below the pea (4).

CORDING

A series of knots worked on the vertical is a braid. When the knots are worked horizontally, it is called a cord. Cording requires the various threads to be 'set on' to a holding cord using a 'lark's head knot'. Pin the holding cord to the knotting board. Cut your working thread to the correct length and fold in half. Slide the folded end under the holding cord (1). Bring the 2 ends of the thread down through the loop, passing them over the holding cord (2). Pull gently on the ends to tighten the knot (3). Set-on threads are usually folded in half in the middle, but they can be folded elsewhere to get 2 threads of different lengths.

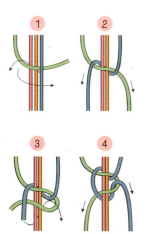

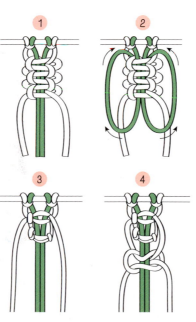

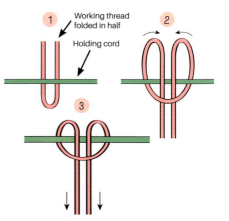

BRAIDED HEADBAND

Easily braided, this chic headband works well with many different outfits.

YOU WILL NEED

▸ 225cm (88½in) of 3mm (⅛in) wide pink suede cord
▸ 18cm (7in) of 1.3cm (½in) wide elastic ribbon
▸ Adhesive tape or masking tape
▸ Needle and pink sewing cotton
▸ Fabric glue
▸ A bulldog clip

STEP BY STEP

1. Cut five 45cm (17¼in) lengths of suede cord. Align and pin each length.

2-3. Follow the steps for the 5-ply plait in Technique 2, page 22.

4. Do not pin the suede cord in the body of the plait, it is better to use adhesive tape to hold the braid in place as you work. Plait a 36cm (14¼in) braid, pulling tight as you go.

5. Remove the braid from the knotting board and wrap adhesive tape around both ends to hold the braid together.

TO FINISH

Cut 18cm (7in) of elastic ribbon. Remove the masking tape and use fabric glue to stick the ends of the braid to the back of the elastic ribbon. Hold the joins together with a bulldog clip. When the glue is completely dry, sew the braid onto the elastic ribbon.

TIE-DYE NECKLACE

A piece of string, a wooden bead... you'll love the simplicity of this unusual necklace.

YOU WILL NEED

- 2m (2yd) cabled cotton twine, 3mm (⅛in) diameter
- A large undyed wooden bead, 2.5cm (1in) diameter
- Navy blue dilutable liquid dye
- Adhesive tape or masking tape

STEP BY STEP

1. Cut 80cm (31½in) of twine. Wrap the ends in masking tape. Slide the wooden bead to the centre of the cord and tie off the necklace with an overhand knot 4cm (1½in) from each end. Mark the bead's position with masking tape.

2-3. Cut a 60cm (23½in) piece of twine, fold in half and slip it under the main thread, 15cm (6in) from the bead.

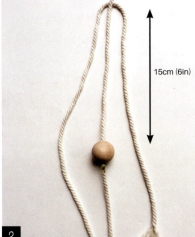

15cm (6in)

4. Braid a 3-ply plait up to the point where the bead is located.

5-6. Tie an overhand knot to finish the braid and slide the bead up to it.

7. Thread the right-hand cord through the knot so it is next to the left-hand cord.

8. Do the same on the other side using another 60cm (23¼in) length of twine. Tie an overhand knot 4cm (1½in) from the end of the necklace to stop the end fraying.

TO FINISH

9. Dilute the dye in a container to achieve the desired shade. Thoroughly soak the 4 cords on either side of the bead and the ends of the main cord in water up to the required height. Dip the ends into the dye: the colour should diffuse naturally up through the wet section over a few hours. Allow to drip dry.

10. Once completely dry, unravel the strands of the cords.

POM-POM BAG TASSEL

A pretty bag scoubidou for big and little girls.

YOU WILL NEED

- 6m (6½yd) black waxed cotton, 2mm (⅛in) diameter
- 30cm (11¾in) turquoise waxed cotton, 1mm (½₅in) diameter
- A key ring
- 4 turquoise glass beads
- Adhesive tape or masking tape

STEP BY STEP

A. Cut four 150cm (59in) lengths of black waxed cotton. Align the stands, then fold and pass the folded end through the key ring to form an 8cm (3¼in) long loop.

1. Wrap the threads in masking tape.

8 cm

A

1

2. Tie a 3cm (1¼in) coil knot around all the threads (see Technique 1, page 8) using a 30cm (11¾in) length of turquoise waxed cotton.

3-4. Place the work vertically and plait a 4-ply braid.

TO FINISH

5-6. When you reach 5cm (2in) from the end of the threads, tie an overhand knot through all the threads to finish the braid. Slide a bead onto each thread and secure with an overhand knot.

CHIC BRACELET

The gold clasps turn this series of flat knots into a very chic accessory. You could make several and wear them together.

YOU WILL NEED

- Two 10cm (4in) long, 10mm (⅜in) wide ribbon clamps
- 10–16 rings, 6mm (¼in) diameter
- 2 round clasps, 6mm (¼in) diameter
- 134cm (52½in) coloured cotton twine, 2mm (¹⁄₁₆in) diameter
- Glue gun
- Jewellery pliers

STEP BY STEP

1. From the cotton twine cut two 45cm (17¼in) lengths (working threads) and four 11cm (4¼in) lengths (leader cords). Position and pin the lengths to your knotting board.

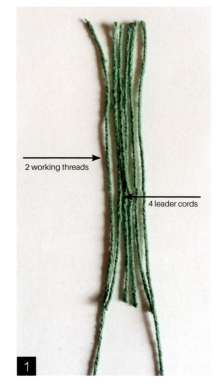

2 working threads

4 leader cords

1

2

2-3-4. Work a braid using 15 flat knots (see Technique 3, page 23). Make sure you keep the 4 leader cords flat.

5. Place the ends of the 2 working threads on top of the leader cords and stick into place with the glue gun. When the glue is completely dry, snip off any excess threads.

TO FINISH

6. Attach the 2 ribbon clamps, then the rings and clasps to fit your wrist.

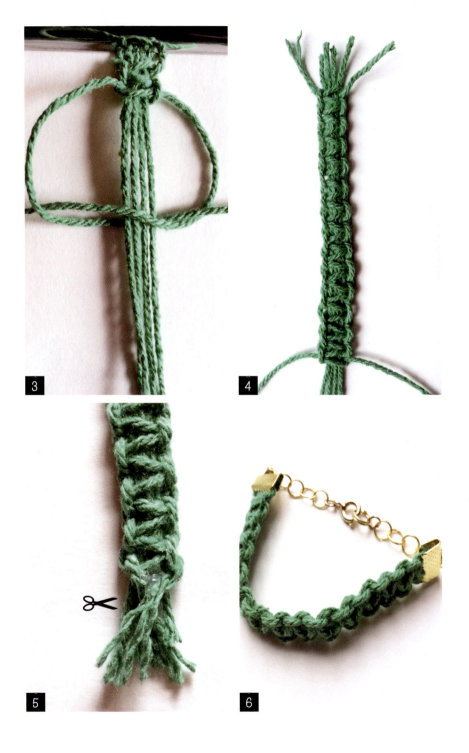

FRIENDSHIP BRACELET

This linen twine and embroidery yarn mix makes a pretty and stylish friendship bracelet.

YOU WILL NEED

- 280cm (110in) linen twine, 2mm (¹⁄₁₆in) diameter
- DMC embroidery yarn, art. 117, no. 4235,4200,4077,4050: 220cm (86½in) of each
- Fabric glue that dries transparent

STEP BY STEP

1. From the linen twine, cut a 60cm (23½in) length (leader cord) and a 220cm (86½in) length (working thread). From each colour of the embroidery yarn, cut a 220cm (86½in) length (working threads). Fold the 60cm (23½in) length of linen twine in half to make 2 leader cords. Leaving a 0.5cm (¼in) long loop in the leader cord, work a flat knot around it starting at the middle of the five 220cm (86½in) lengths. The loop will form part of the clasp. Divide the threads as follows: the 2 leader cords (the shorter ones) in the centre and on either side: 1 linen twine thread and 4 embroidery yarn threads.

2. Work flat knots (see Technique 3, page 23) for about 16cm (6¼in), depending on how long you want the bracelet to be.

TO FINISH

3-4. Tie all the threads together in 2 overhand knots on top of each other. Pull tight.

5. Snip threads off to the desired length and use fabric glue to hold in them in place.

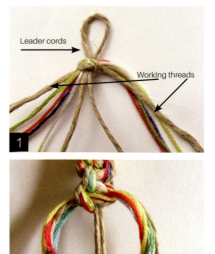

EPAULETTES

Customise a jacket, shirt or plain dress with these unusual and striking shoulder designs.

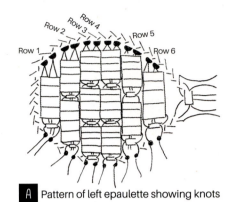

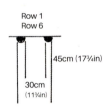
A Pattern of left epaulette showing knots

YOU WILL NEED

▶ 26m (28yd) Hoooked Zpagetti jersey yarn, art 800/ MIXMARINE
▶ A small crochet hook or thin wooden stick
▶ Two 3cm (1¼in) long safety pin
▶ Brooch pin

STEP BY STEP

1-B. Cut three 65cm (25½in) lengths of yarn. Align them and tie a collecting knot 10cm (4in) along (see Technique 1, page 8). Plait the 3 threads (see Technique 2, page 22) for 28cm (11in) and tie off the braid using a temporary overhand knot.

Left epaulette
Row one: for the first row, cut two 75cm (29½in) lengths and fold them in two to the lengths shown in (**B**).

2-A. Set the 2 lengths onto the plait using a lark's head knot with the loop going from top to bottom (**A**). The plait becomes the holding cord.

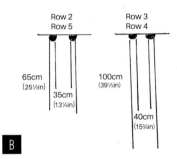

B

1

3-4-5-6. Form a pea knot by working a braid of 4 flat knots turned in on themselves (see Technique 3, page 23). The leader cords pass between the 2 threads coming down from the lark's head knot. You can use a hook to help pull the yarn through. Tie off the pea knot with a tight flat knot.

C. Attach the 2 working threads to the other side of the plait. Let the ends of the yarn hang down.

7. Row 2: set on two 100cm (39½in) lengths folded in two as (**B**) and set them on next to the first pea on the plait (**A**). Work 2 pea knots, of 4 flat knots each. Tie the braid onto the plait.

8-9. Row 3: cut two 140cm (55in) lengths and fold them in two (**B**). Then attach them as in (**A**). Make 3 pea knots, of 4 flat knots each, and attach them to the plait.
Row 4: continue as for row 3.
Row 5: continue as for row 2.
Row 6: continue as for row 1.

10. Undo the temporary overhand knot in the plait and make a flat knot using the 4 central threads (leaving the outside threads to the side).

Right epaulette
Proceed as for the left epaulette by setting the lengths of yarn to the left of the middle of the plait.

2

3

C

7

11

12

The 2 leader cords pass between each set of threads from the lark's head knot

4

5

6

8

9

10

13

TO FINISH

11. Using a small wooden stick or crochet hook, push the leader threads from the pea knots through the last lark's head knots on the braid.

12. Sew a brooch pin onto the back of each epaulette.

13. Cut the fringes to the desired length. In the photo it is 6cm (2½in).

TECHNIQUE 4

TWIST KNOTS

A twist knot is a repetition of the first half of a flat knot. After the first few knots, the rest start to form a twisting pattern.

LEFT-HAND TWIST KNOT

A twist knot is formed from 2 threads worked around one or more leader cords. The leader cords will be the same length as the completed project, while the working threads should be 5 times longer. It is basically a repeated series of the first part of a flat knot. Repeat stages 1 to 3. Push the knots upwards. The spiral pattern will form itself.

DOUBLE TWIST KNOT

Making a double twist is more complex than the twist knot and requires a bit of practice. Tie the middle of the 2 working threads around the leader cords (1). Bring the strands of the lower threads upwards, under the other thread on the left-hand side and over the other strand on the right-hand side (2). Tie a twist knot (3). Bring the strands of the lower threads upwards, over on the left-hand side and under on the right (4). Tie a twist knot (5). You have made a double twist. Continue in the same way, repeating stages 1 to 5. As the work spirals, continue knotting as before.

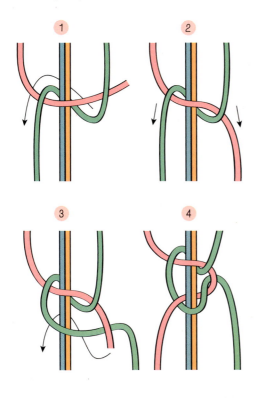

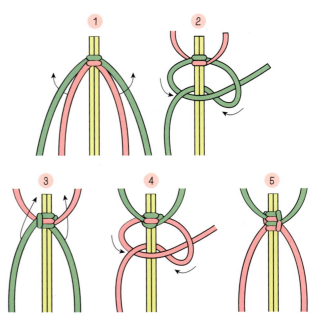

TECHNIQUE 5

ALTERNATE FLAT KNOT

Alternate flat knots are staggered row by row, to create a 'web'. This commonly used pattern is one of the most decorative.

ALTERNATE FLAT KNOTS

The appearance of the finished webs made from alternating flat knots varies depending on the number of flat knots used and the space between the rows. Spacing between rows must be regular. You can use a strip of cardboard cut to the right height to help you to space the rows evenly.

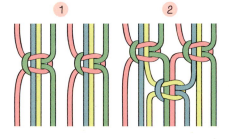

TECHNIQUE 6

CORDS

Cords form lines of knots used in the macramé techniques known as micro-macramé and Cavandoli.

Cords are a series of semi-interlocking half-hitches made on a holding cord. The holding cord can be a separate thread or one of the lengths that has already been set on. Cording means you can make lines (horizontal, diagonal, slanting) and geometric shapes (diamonds, Xs, Vs, inverted Vs, zigzags). Cording can be done from left to right and right to left.

HORIZONTAL CORD

The holding cord runs horizontally and the working cords run vertically. The working cord is knotted from left to right (1–2) or right to left (3–4). The working threads are knotted one by one to obtain this result (5). By alternating horizontal cords from right to left and from left to right, you obtain a solid panel (6).

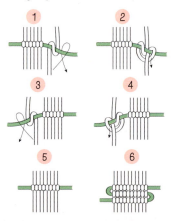

DIAGONAL CORD

This works on the same principle as a horizontal cord but in this case the holding cord is set on a diagonal. The knots are worked on a holding cord that runs right to left (1–2) or left to right (3–4). Completed horizontal cord (5) and series of zigzag cords (6).

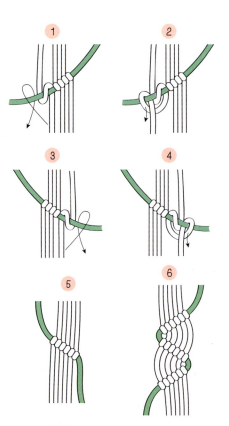

TWO-TONE TWISTED BRACELET

A pearl cotton bracelet with a sparkling streak of precious silver thread.

YOU WILL NEED

▶ DMC pearl cotton art.115-3 no. 310, no. 415
▶ 1 silver DMC embroidery yarn no. E168
▶ Metal clasp set
▶ Hot-melt glue gun

STEP BY STEP

1. Cut two 130cm (51in) lengths of cotton no. 310, two 130cm (51in) lengths of cotton no. 415, one 130cm (51in) length of embroidery yarn no. E168. Cut a 40cm (15¾in) length of cotton no. 310 for the leader cord.

2. Fold the 40cm (15¾in) length in half and pin it to your knotting board. Instead of knotting 2 threads twice, here the twist is made with two lots of 2 threads and two lots of 3 threads. Align the two 130cm (51in) lengths of no. 415 with the 130cm (51in) length of embroidery yarn, folded in two and tied using an overhand knot around the leader cords.

3-4-5-6-7-8. Align the two 130cm (51in) lengths of no. 310 and fold in half. Use an overhand knot to tie them onto the holding cords under the previous threads.

9. Work twist knots for 15cm (6in), alternating the colours.

10. Finish with a collecting knot. Trim short. Use the glue gun to stick the ends together and push quickly into the cord end on the clasp.

BOHO NECKLACE

This necklace uses undyed materials and requires little effort to achieve an original boho-chic effect.

YOU WILL NEED

▶ 690cm (272in) cabled cotton twine, 1.5mm (¹⁄₁₆in) diameter

▶ 290cm (114in) natural crochet yarn, 1mm (¹⁄₂₅in) diameter

▶ 75 wooden beads, 1cm (¹⁄₄in) diameter

▶ Untreated wood bead, 1.5cm (½in) diameter

STEP BY STEP

1. Cut a 250cm (98in) length of cabled cotton twine, 1.5mm (¹⁄₁₆in) in diameter. Fold in half to make a loop and 2 leader cords. Fix securely to your knotting board. Cut the first length of crochet yarn 200cm (79in) in length, 1mm (¹⁄₂₅in) in diameter. It will be easy to add threads as you are working 200cm (79in) lengths folded in half (200cm/79in allows for a 9.5cm/3¾in-long twist). Knot the first length 1.5cm (½in) from the top, followed by tight twist knots for 25cm (9¾in) (see Technique 4, page 44).

2. The twist will start to spiral naturally after 10 knots. It doesn't make any difference if you placed the thread to the left or right to work the knot. Cut a new 200cm (79in) length of natural crochet yarn folded in half and continue as before. Hide the previous ends of threads under the new twist.

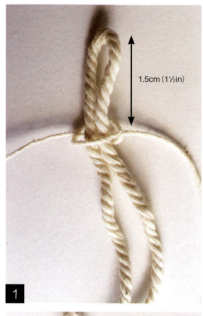

1.5cm (1½in)

First thread

Second thread

3-4. Cut thirty 30cm (11¾in) lengths of 1mm (⅟₂₅in) crochet yarn. When you are 25cm (9¾in) along the twist, insert two 30cm (11¾in) threads folded in half through the last twist knot.

5. Wrap a piece of adhesive tape round the end of these 4 pieces to make threading on the beads easier.

6. Thread on 3 treated beads, separating them with an overhand knot (see Technique 1, pages 8–9). Tie a 25cm (9¾in) twist knot to finish.

7. Repeat 15 times, at 3cm (1¼in) intervals.

TO FINISH

8. Tie an overhand knot with all the threads in the twist. Slide on the untreated 1.5mm (⅟₁₆in) bead and tie another overhand knot.

9-10. Trim the crochet yarn beaded lengths to 3.5cm (1¼in). Comb out the strands to create a tassel effect.

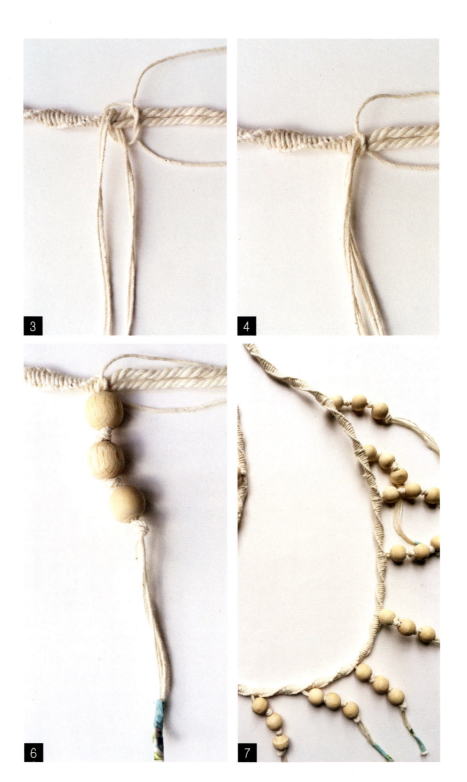

5

8 Starting loop — End bead

9

10

TOTE BAG

This tote uses twist knots to the left to create an unusual effect.
The dimensions of the finished bag are 22.5 x 26cm (8³⁄₄ x 10¹⁄₄in).

YOU WILL NEED

▶ 70m (76yd) apple green jute twine, 2mm (¹⁄₁₆in) diameter
▶ Fabric glue
▶ Adhesive tape or masking tape

STEP BY STEP

The tote consists of a front and back worked as one long panel and two handles. Front and back will be attached along line 1. The threads used to work the handles will also be used to tie the twists of lines 3–7 and 12–16 of the body of the bag.

Handles

Cut four 85cm (33½in) lengths and four 330cm (130in) lengths of twine. This is 2 pieces for each handle.

A. For each of the handles, place the lengths as shown. Lay the two 330cm (130in) lengths flat. When you are 100cm (39½in) from the end, lay the two 85cm (33½in) lengths parallel to and between the other two.

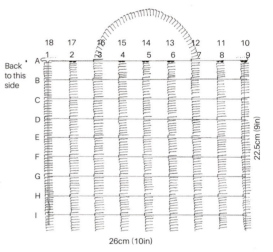

Pattern: Enlarge by 250 percent

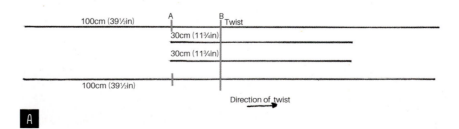

1-A. Wrap a strip of adhesive tape around the 4 threads at point B, 30cm (11¾in) from point A.

2-3-4-B. Work a 20cm (7¼in) length of twist knots tied to the left (see Technique 4, page 44); this will be about 50 knots. Put to one side.

Bag panels

Cut twenty-six 160cm (63in) lengths (threads for lines 2, 4, 5, 6, 8, 9, 10, 11, 13, 14, 15, 17 and 18). Cut one 220cm (87in) length (line 1 leader cords) and one 135cm (53in) thread (leader cord A and line 1 leader cords).

Assembling the panels

Place the pattern on your knotting board. Pin the 135cm (53in) length onto the pattern along line 1 and row A. This will form one of the holding cords for line 1 and the leader cord for row A of the front.

Front

C. Row A: each group of two 160cm (63in) threads will be placed alternately.

5-6. Set on lark's head knots, loop down, on lines 2, 4, 5, 6, 8 and 9. Tie a series of 6 twist knots. Make sure you pull the first knot tight to hold the lark's head knot in place. The work will start to twist from the 5th knot. Continue.

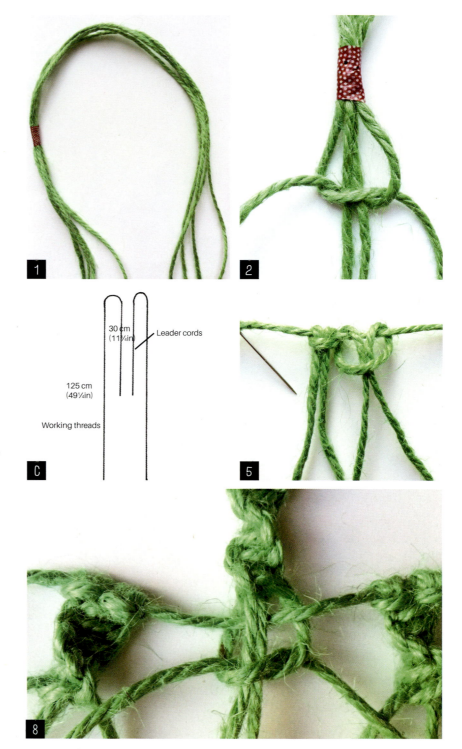

1

2

30 cm
(11¾in)

Leader cords

125 cm
(49¼in)

Working threads

C

5

8

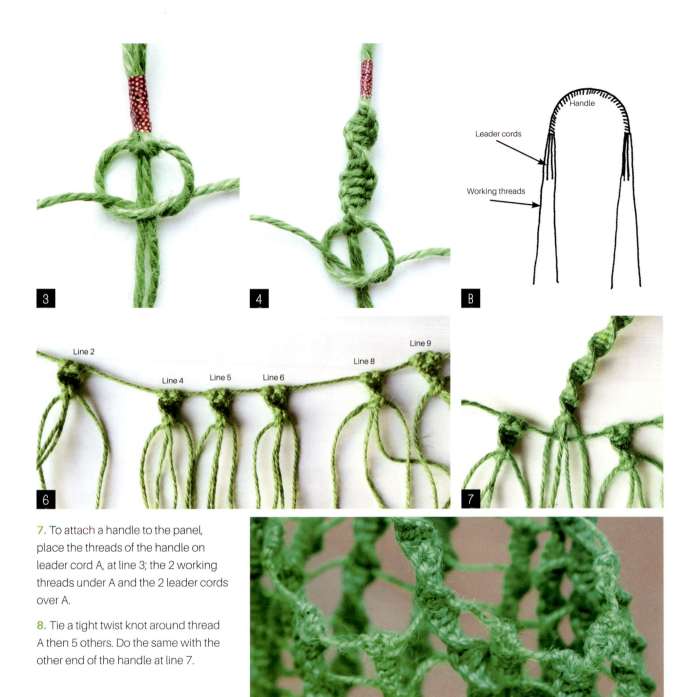

3

4

B

Handle

Leader cords

Working threads

Line 2   Line 4   Line 5   Line 6   Line 8   Line 9

6

7

7. To attach a handle to the panel, place the threads of the handle on leader cord A, at line 3; the 2 working threads under A and the 2 leader cords over A.

8. Tie a tight twist knot around thread A then 5 others. Do the same with the other end of the handle at line 7.

9. Row B: cut a 120cm (47¼in) length. Keeping back the first 30cm (11¾in), place the length over the working threads and under the leader cords of each line.

10. Work a twist including thread B, on lines 2 to 9. Then tie 6 other twist knots on each line. Continue in the same way for the following rows using the following measurements:

Row C: cut a 100cm (39½in) length. Keep back 23cm (9in).

Row D: cut a 90cm (35½in) length. Keep back 21cm (8¼in).

Row E: cut a 83cm (32¾in) length. Keep back 18cm (7in).

Row F: cut a 80cm (31½in) length. Keep back 16cm (6¼in).

Row G: cut a 73cm (28¾in) length. Keep back 14cm (5½in).

Row H: cut a 68cm (26¾in) length. Keep back 11cm (4¼in).

Row I: cut a 60cm (23½in) length. Keep back 6cm (2½in).

Back

11. Fold your work towards the left so line 9 is located 2cm (¾in) to the left of line 1. Set on two 135cm (53in) lengths as shown in diagram 3 on lines 10, 11, 13, 14, 15, 17 and 18. Attach handle to holding cord A at line no. 11 and 15 with a twist knot taking in thread A. For each of the lines, make a 6-knot twist and include a 7th knot in rows B to I.

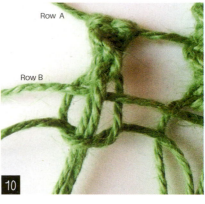

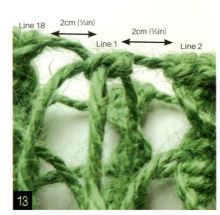

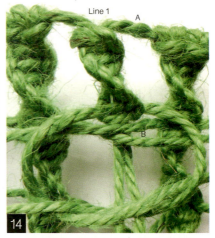

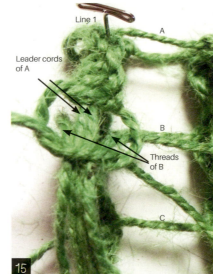

Line 9 · Line 10 · Line 11 · Line 13 · Line 14 · Line 15 · etc.

11

12

TO FINISH

12. Position the bag as shown. The 2 ends of holding cord A become the leader cords of line 1.

13. Work the 200cm (79in) length, folded in half 2cm (¾in) from line 18 and 2, into a twist.

14. Tie a series of 6 twist knots. On the 7th knot, work in the 2 ends of row B. Make sure this knot is pulled tight.

15. The next two knots will take in the threads from row B and the leader cords of A, namely 4 leader cords. Trim short the ends of thread B. Continue until the bottom of the bag. Make sure you do not cut off the wrong thread. To be on the safe side, tie a simple 'reminder' knot at the ends of the threads to be trimmed.

16. Turn the bag right sides together. Finish the bottom of the bag by tying twist knots using the leader cords of the front and back twists: the 2 threads from the back will be used as working threads round the 2 threads from the front. Glue the knots and trimmed threads using transparent fabric glue. Wait until the glue is completely dry before turning the bag the right way out.

TURQUOISE CUFF

A beautiful cuff-style bracelet created using traditional macramé latticework.

YOU WILL NEED
For a 16.5cm (6½in) cuff (not including clasp)

▸ 960cm (378in) waxed cotton twine, 1mm (1/25in) diameter
▸ Piece of card, 1cm (½in) high
▸ White vinyl glue
▸ 10mm (3/8in) ribbon clasp
▸ Jewellery pliers
▸ Small glue brush

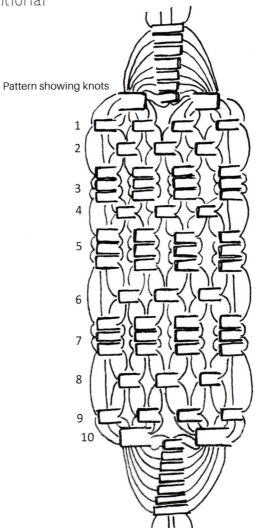

Pattern showing knots

1
2

3
4

5

6

7

8

9
10

STEP BY STEP

1. Cut sixteen 60cm (23½in) lengths of twine. Separate the lengths into 4 groups of 4 threads. Tie an overhand knot 15cm (6in) from the top of the threads, (see Technique 1, page 8) for each of the groups. Fix the whole thing securely to your knotting board.

Row 1: 1.5cm (½in) from the overhand knots, tie a flat knot with each group of 4 threads (see Technique 5, page 45).

2-3. Row 2: put the first 2 threads to one side and knot 3 flat knots, offset to alternate the pattern from row 1, 1cm (½in) from row 1. Use the piece of card to help you to space the rows evenly.

4. Row 3: Continue alternating the knots, but creating a braid of 3 flat knots.
Row 4: continue as for row 2.
Row 5: continue as for row 3.
Row 6: continue as for row 2.
Row 7: continue as for row 3.
Row 8: continue as for row 2.
Row 9: continue as for row 1.

5. Row 10: make 2 groups of 8 threads.

6. Tie a flat knot with 2 lots of 2 working threads and 4 leader cords, just below row 9. Turn the work over. Undo the temporary knots and work as you did row 10.

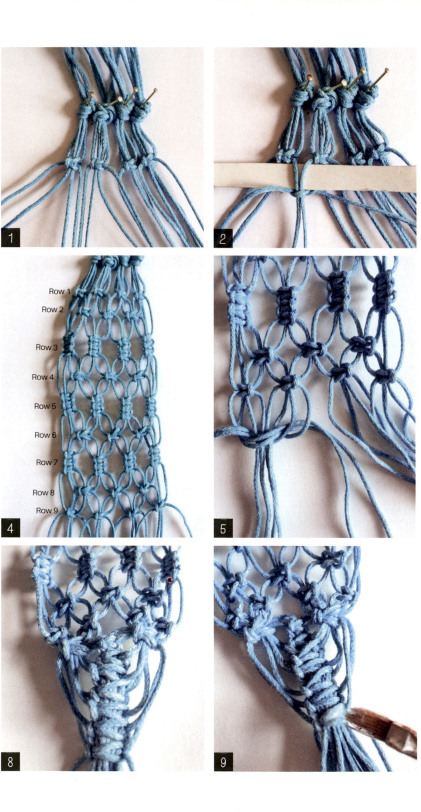

TO FINISH

7. To bring the threads into a single braid, tie a series of 7 flat knots starting with the 4 middle threads.

8. Each subsequent flat knot will use all the threads from the previous knots as leader cords. Do the same at the other end.

9. Hold the threads in place with some vinyl glue.

10. Once completely dry, trim the threads. Place both ends in the clasp and squeeze the clasp shut with the jewellery pliers. To avoid marking the clasp with the pliers, slip a piece of material between the clasp and the pliers.

BIB NECKLACE

Give a simple T-shirt a stylish new look with this fringed jersey yarn bib necklace.

YOU WILL NEED

▶ 40m (44yd) XL beige Hoooked Zpagetti jersey yarn
▶ A T-shirt with a round neck
▶ Needle and beige cotton thread
▶ Bulldog clip

STEP BY STEP

1. Cut a 50cm (19¾in) length of yarn that will act as the holding cord. Cut twenty 200cm (79in) lengths. Fold the yarn in half and knot the 20 pieces onto the holding cord.

2. Trace the T-shirt's neckline onto a piece of paper so you can follow the curve. Centre the holding cord on this line and fix it into place on the knotting board. Separate the lengths into 5 groups. The lengths should be distributed as follows: 8-4-16-4-8.

3. Then divide the lengths into the first three groups of 8 strands – 4 strands with a knot at the beginning and a group of16 strands.

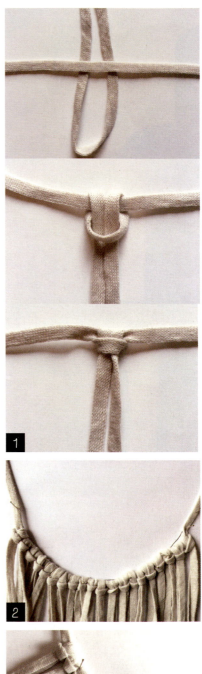

4. Row 1: leaving aside the groups of 8 strands, work pea knots with the 2 groups of 4 strands (strands 9–12 and 29–32). This will mean working a braid of 3 flat knots (**3**) and turning them in on themselves (see Technique 3, page 23). Tie a flat knot under the pea knot to hold it firmly in place. Tie 4 tight flat knots with the group of 16 strands between the 2 pea knots.

5. Row 2: set aside the 2 outside strands under the pea knots, and work 5 flat knots offset in a staggered pattern in relation to the knots in row 1. **Row 3**: set aside the first 8 and last 8 strands; tie 6 flat knots.

6. Row 4: bring strands 7–8 and 33–34 into the panel and tie 7 alternate flat knots. **Row 5**: set aside the first 2 and last 2 strands of row 4 and work 6 flat knots offset in a staggered pattern in relation to the knots in the previous row. **Row 6**: tie 7 flat knots. **Row 7**: bring in strands 5–6 and 35–36 and work 8 alternate flat knots. **Row 8**: work 7 flat knots. **Row 9**: work 8 flat knots. **Row 10**: bring in strands 3–4 and 33–34 and work 9 alternate flat knots. **Row 11**: work 8 flat knots. **Row 12**: work 9 flat knots. **Row 13**: bring in strands 1–2 and 39–40. Form a pea knot by working a braid of 3 flat knots turned in on themselves as in row 1. Tie 8 flat knots between the two pea knots.

7. Rows 14-21: work flat knots reducing by one knot at the start and end of each row.

8. Row 22: make a braid of 3 flat knots and turn it in on itself to form a pea knot. Finish with a flat knot underneath it to hold it in place.

9. Cut the ends off on a diagonal to a length of 7cm (2¾in).

10. Sew the holding cord to the neck of the T-shirt.

NET SHOPPING BAG

My shopping bag? I made it myself actually...
using natural and navy blue jute.

YOU WILL NEED

▸ 102m (111yd) natural jute twine,
  2mm (1/16in) diameter
▸ 10m (11yd) navy blue jute twine,
  2mm (1/16in) diameter
▸ Bulldog clip
▸ Hot-melt glue gun

STEP BY STEP

The bag comprises 2 plaited handles
and 2 sides of staggered knots,
assembled as you go along.

HANDLES

Cut 12 pieces of natural jute twine,
100cm (39½in) in length. Divide into
2 groups of 6 lengths.

1. Align a group of 6 lengths, pulling
one 2cm (¾in) above the others.

2. Using this length, make a collecting
knot (see Technique 1, page 8) with
one of the strands around the 5 others,
4cm (1½in) from the end.

3. Attach to your knotting board and
make a 3-ply plait (see Technique 2,
page 22) with 3 lots of 2 strands until
4cm (1½in) from the other end. End the
plait with a collecting knot. Repeat for
the second handle. Make sure the
plaits are the same length.

4. Cut 2 pieces of natural jute twine, 25cm (9¾in) in length. Make a circle with the plait and place the collecting knots side by side. Tie a coil knot (see Technique 1, page 8) on each handle. Cut off any strands that are longer than the others.

BAG FRONT

5. Cut 18 pieces of natural jute twine, and 2 pieces of navy blue, 2.5m (2¾yd) in length. Fold the 18 lengths in half, and set them onto one of the handles, distributed as follows ('n' for natural and 'b' for navy blue):
2n-2n-2n-2n-2b-2n-2n-2n-2n.
Set each group of 2 threads onto the coil knot created previously, spaced 1cm (¼in) apart.

6. Row 1: set aside the first 4 threads (1-2-3-4) and the last 4 threads (33-34-35-36). They will be used to plait the border. Work 7 tight flat knots.

7. At the first and last flat knot, incorporate one of the threads to make the border plait: the strand on the far left for the right-hand knot and the strand on the far right for the left-hand knot.

Row 2: set aside the first 6 and last 6 strands. Work 6 flat knots, staggering them in relation to the flat knots in row 1 (2cm/¾in below row 1).

8. Braid the 6 strands that were set aside into a 3-ply plait (3 groups of 2 strands), on each side, up to the level of row 3. Use a bulldog clip to stop the plaits unravelling.

9. Row 3: set aside the first 4 and last 4 threads of the plait. The 2 remaining threads of the plaits will work the neighbouring flat knots. Work 7 knots, staggering them in relation to row 2.

10. Row 4: continue as for row 2. Continue the plait.
Row 5: continue as for row 3.
Row 6: continue as for row 2. Continue the plait.

Row 7: continue as for row 3. Continue the 2 plaits until this point and finish them with an overhand knot.

BAG BACK

Cut 18 lengths of natural jute twine, and 2 lengths of navy blue, 2.5m (2¾yd) in length. Fold the 18 lengths in half. Repeat all stages from row 1 to row 7.

11. Row 8: To attach the front to the back, place the pieces side by side.

6

7

Row 1

29 30 31 32 33 34 35 36

10

Row 1
Row 2
Row 3
Row 4
Row 5
Row 6
Row 7

11

12. Identify the two outermost strands on each side.

13. Work a flat knot between the front and back.

14. Reposition the front and back as shown in the photo.

15. Rows 9–23: from this point on, you will always be working 'in a tube'.
Row 24: tie a row of alternate flat knots, but as close as possible to row 23.

16. Knotting the bottom of the bag
Turn the bag inside out, right sides together. Work flat knots using 2 strands from the front knot and 2 from the back knot, right along the bottom. Tie double flat knots for extra strength. Pull the knots tight. Trim the strands to 10mm (⅜in) from the knot and stick as cleanly as possible with the glue gun.

17. When the glue is completely dry, turn the bag the right way out.

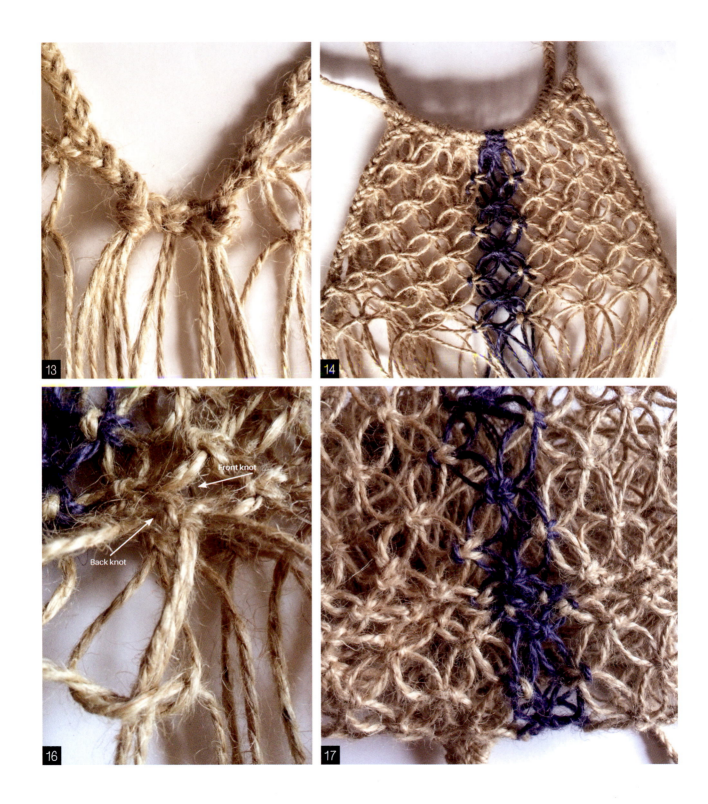

13

14

16

Front knot

Back knot

17

RETRO BELT

This diamond-patterned belt is inspired by the 1970s but is right on-trend today.

YOU WILL NEED
For a 160cm (63in) belt (small)

▶ 36m (40yd) off-white waxed cotton cord, 1.5mm (1/16in) diameter

For each dress size increase (medium, large etc), add 50cm (19¾in) off-white waxed cotton cord and 2 diamonds.

STEP BY STEP

1. Cut 12 pieces of waxed cotton, 320m (350yd) in length. Align the ends and start working 20cm (7¾in) from one end. Tie an overhand knot on each of the ends. Tie all 12 strands together using a temporary overhand knot.

2. Divide the strands into 3 groups of 4 strands each. Work a braid using 4 flat knots (see Technique 5, page 45).

3. Divide the 12 strands into 2 groups of 6 strands each.
Row 1: strand 6 will act as the holding cord for a diagonal cord from right to left with the 5 left-hand strands (see Technique 6, page 45).
Row 2: strand 7 will act as the holding cord for a diagonal cord from left to right with the 5 remaining strands.

4. Rows 3–4: the 2 holding cords act as holding cords for the ensuing diagonals which will form a 4cm (1½in) high diamond. The left-hand holding cord is knotted in the same way over the right-hand holding cord.

5. Row 5: continue the slanting cord from right to left by knotting the next 5 strands.

Row 6: take the holding cord from row 3 and work a slanting cord from left to right.

6. Repeat rows 3-4-5-6 to form 14 diamonds.

7. Divide the strands into 3 groups of 4 strands each. Knot a braid using 4 flat knots as you did at the beginning.

8. Trim the strands to 20cm (7¾in) and tie an overhand knot at the end of each strand. Undo the temporary overhand knot that you started with.

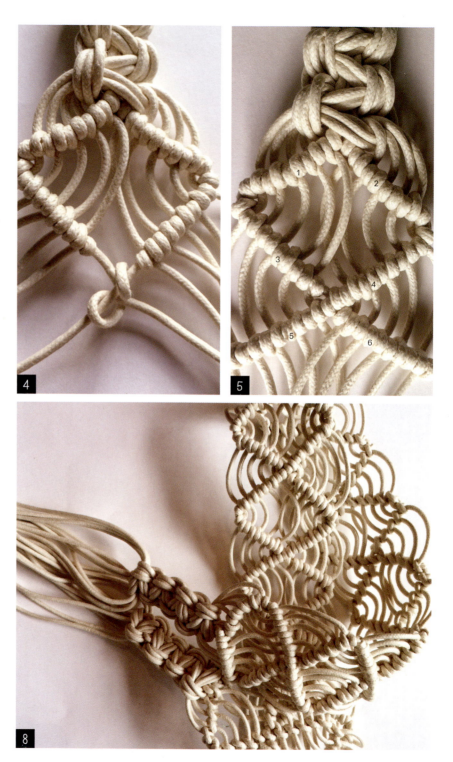

6

7

BLUE SNOOD

This snood is revisited in cotton jersey for a dramatic modern style.

YOU WILL NEED

- 42m (46yd) of DMC Hoooked Zpagetti jersey yarn art. 800 in navy blue
- Fabric glue

STEP BY STEP

A. Cut a 620cm (244in) length of yarn to act as the holding cord and to form some of the structure. Fold in two and pin onto your knotting board as shown.

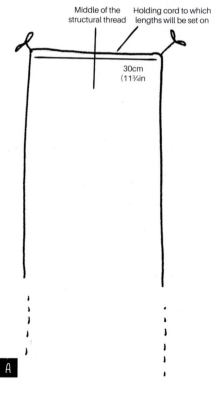

Middle of the structural thread

Holding cord to which lengths will be set on

30cm (11¾in)

A

1-2. Cut nineteen 160cm (63in) lengths of yarn, fold them in half and set the strands onto the horizontal part of the holding cord.

B. Cut a 610cm (240in) length of yarn, fold it as shown and set it on last, to the right-hand side of the holding cord. This will act as the leader cord for the cords throughout the work.

3. Row 1: knot an initial horizontal cord from right to left, right against the knots on the holding cord, leaving the structural yarn to one side (see Technique 6, page 45).

4. Work a cord from left to right, then from right to left every 10cm (4in) for 80cm (31½in), always using the same leader cord. Knot onto the structural thread each time you pass it.

5. When the snood reaches a length of 80cm (31½in), fold it right sides together. Pass 10cm (4in) of each strand between the initial lark's head knots.

6. Fix in place using fabric glue. Once fully dry, trim off any surplus and turn the snood the right way out.

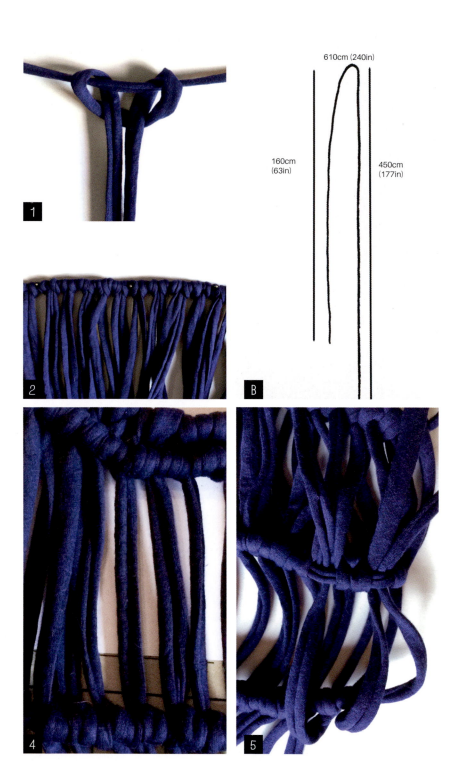

610cm (240in)

160cm (63in)

450cm (177in)

Mounting knots

Thread no. 40
leader cord

Structural
thread

3

6

VEST TOP STRAPS

Make your very own customised lace macramé straps to perk up a simple vest top.

YOU WILL NEED

▶ A vest top
▶ 38m (41yd) cotton twine, 1mm (¹⁄₂₅in) diameter, in a colour to match the vest
▶ Sewing needle and cotton thread in a matching colour
▶ A yarn needle with a large eye

Pattern showing knots

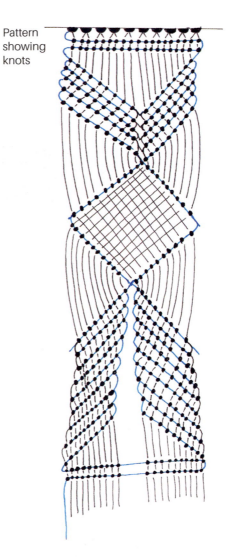

STEP BY STEP (FOR ONE STRAP)

1. Cut a 15cm (6in) length of twine for the holding cord. Wrap adhesive tape around the ends to make it easier to pin to your knotting board. Cut eleven 170cm (67in) lengths of twine. Fold in half and set onto the holding cord.

2. The first strand acts as the leader thread for the first 2 rows.

Row 1: work a horizontal cord from left to right (see Technique 6, page 45).

Row 2: work a cord from right to left using the same leader thread.

3. Rows 3–7: separate the strands into 2 groups and work a series of diagonal cords. The outside strands act as leader threads. Work into the angle so that the V measures 2cm (¾in) in height.

4. Bring the left-hand and right-hand cords from each row around each other, as shown. Work 5 diagonal cords on each side.

5. Rows 6–10: form a woven diamond by extending the last cord on the right into a diagonal cord towards the bottom left. Then knot a diagonal cord towards the bottom right starting from the centre.

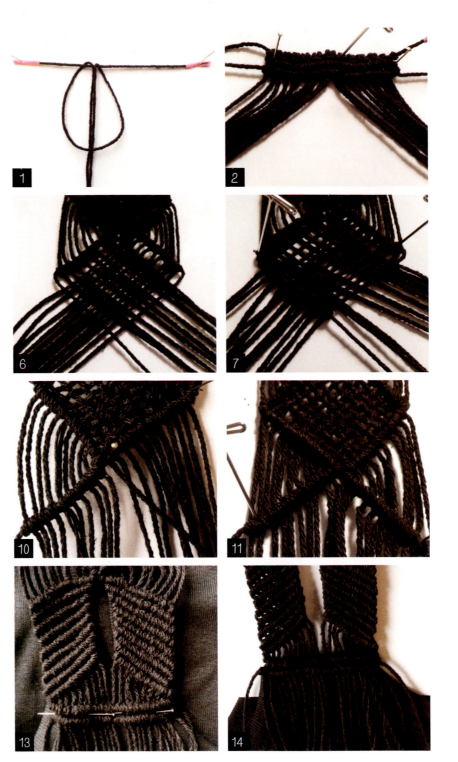

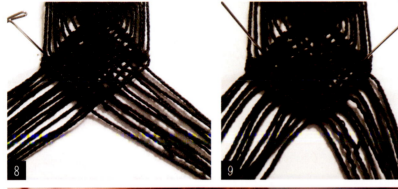

6. Cross the strands of the left-hand cord over the strands of the right-hand cord.

7. Place the next holding cord over the strands and knot a diagonal cord towards the bottom right.

8. Weave the threads over and under using the yarn needle.

9. Knot on the diagonal towards the bottom left to close the diamond.

10. Separate the threads into 2 groups, starting from the 2 central strands that are now holding cords. Work 2 diagonal cords from the centre to the bottom left...

11. ... and from the centre to the bottom right.

12. Form 8 other diagonal cords, then 2 horizontal cords with the leader cord. Repeat all stages for the second strap.

13. Place the straps on the vest top. Mark where the first strap will be attached at the front and back and cut off the original vest straps.

14. Stitch the new straps onto the vest between the horizontal cords.

TECHNIQUE 7

MICRO MACRAMÉ

As its name indicates, micro macramé is like macramé but on a smaller scale. It is particularly good for jewellery. It uses mostly cords.

VERTICAL CORDS

Pass the working thread around the first leader cord (1). Bring the thread around the same leader cord again (2), and pull tight. The vertical cords are worked from right to left (1–2) and from left to right (3–4). Once you have tied the first knot (5), do the same on the second leader cord. At the end of the row, bring the working thread around and knot a cord in the other direction (6).

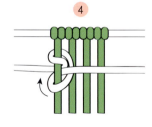

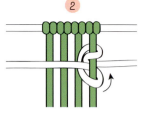

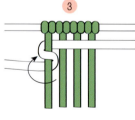

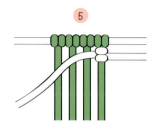

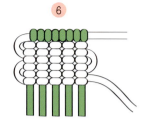

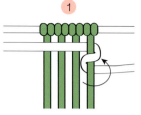

TECHNIQUE 8

CAVANDOLI MACRAMÉ

Cavandoli is a variation that uses half-hitch cording in the form of a panel of embroidery in alternating horizontal and vertical cords, or circular or even 3-D macramé.

THE KNOTS

In this form of circular macramé, you tie half-hitches as you would for diagonal cords. In this case, the leader threads form a spiral. The working threads are worked along the spiral. As in crochet, the dimensions of the piece will vary depending on increases and decreases.

To increase, you add a thread folded in two as shown in the diagram below. To decrease, you simply miss making a knot in the working thread. A circle in a spiral grows gradually bigger, so in order for the piece to remain flat, you need to make any increases as soon as they are necessary.

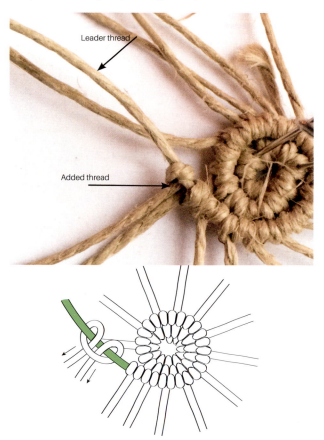

Leader thread

Added thread

HOOP EARRINGS

These navy blue and copper hoop earrings
are an ideal introduction to micro macramé.

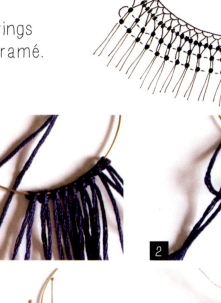

Pattern showing knots

YOU WILL NEED

▶ DMC blue embroidery yarn art. 117
  no. 823
▶ DMC copper embroidery yarn art. 117
  no. E301
▶ Gold hoop earring mounts
▶ Fabric glue

STEP BYSTEP (FOR ONE HOOP)

1. Cut twenty 15cm (6in) lengths of blue
yarn no. 823. Fold in half.

2. Set on to the hoop, loop down.

3. Cut a 120cm (47¼in) piece of copper
yarn. Pin the end firmly to the left-hand side
of the knotting board. Pass it around the
first leader thread. Pin.

4. Row 1: work a vertical cord from left
to right, on each thread.

5. Rows 2–3: work a vertical cord from
right to left, then from left to right over
2 threads.

6. Fix the ends of the working threads
into place at the back using the fabric
glue. Trim the blue threads to a length
of 3cm (1¼in) and unpick the thread
strands to give volume.

GOLD BEAD NECKLACE

A stunning necklace with gold bead decoration that is guaranteed to be admired.

YOU WILL NEED

▸ 27m (29yd) natural cotton crochet yarn, 1mm (¹⁄₂₅in) in diameter
▸ Gold chain
▸ 28 gold-coloured beads, 3mm (¹⁄₈in) diameter
▸ Needle with large eye

STEP BY STEP

1. Cut thirty 80cm (31½in) lengths of yarn. Fold in half and set on to the chain (see Technique 6, page 45).

2. Cut a 120cm (47¼in) length of yarn and pin it to the left of the work. This length is the new holding cord.
Row 1: work a horizontal cord on the holding cord from left to right.
Row 2: work a horizontal cord from right to left with the same holding cord.

3. Separate the threads into 2 groups.

4. Using the same holding cord, work diagonal cords to form a V shape.

5. Thread 9 beads onto strands 30 and 31 before finishing off the V.

6. Use the 1st strand on the left and knot a diagonal cord parallel to the previous one, over 15 threads. Do the same thing from the other side using the last strand as a holding cord.

7. Make 2 new diagonal cords after threading a bead onto strands 2, 14, 48 and 59.

8. Making a diamond. Strands 30 and 31, onto which you have threaded beads, will now act as holding cords. Separate the threads into 4 groups of 15. Work a diagonal cord from the centre to the bottom left and another to the bottom right, both using 15 strands. Thread on a gold bead at the end of the cords.

9. Complete the diamond by working additional diagonal cords. Thread a bead onto each holding cord.

10. Pin out a new 40cm (15¾in) holding cord and work a horizontal cord from left to right, then from right to left, using all the threads.

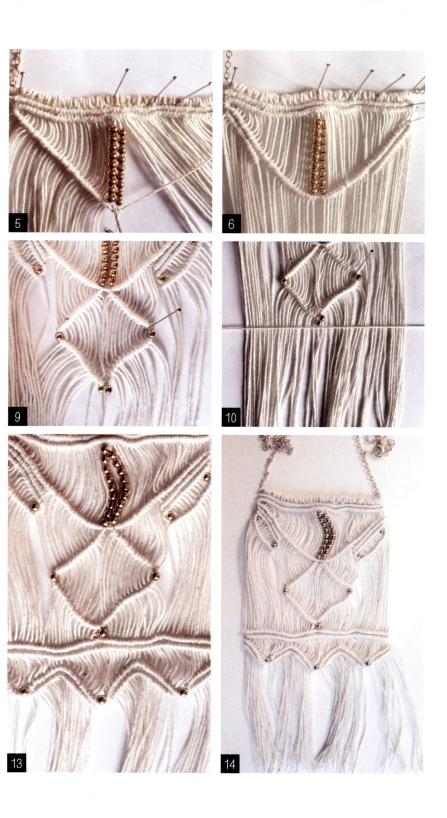

11. Repeat with another 40cm (15¾in) holding cord.

12. Divide the strands into 6 groups of 10 strands each. Pin out a new 60cm (23½in) holding cord. Knot a zigzag cord with 10 strands in each direction. Thread on a bead before each change of direction.

13. Double up the zigzag cord from right to left using the same holding cord.

TO FINISH

14. Using the needle with a large eye, thread the ends of the holding cords through to the back of the work into the knots. Trim off the fringe to a length of 8cm (3¼in).

LEAF CHOKER

Leaf motifs are a micro-macramé classic. I've put five together to make a pretty and unusual choker.

YOU WILL NEED

▶ 1 choker mount, 14cm (5½in) diameter
▶ Embroidery yarn DMC art. 89 no. 2595, 2139, 2644, 2104, 2741 x 1
▶ Fabric glue

STEP BY STEP

1. For each leaf: set on seven 60cm (23½in) lengths of embroidery yarn folded in half in the middle.

2. Leave the 1st thread to one side.

3. From rows 1–7: work a horizontal cord.
Row 2: leave the 1st strand to one side and work a horizontal cord (see Technique 6, page 45). The last knot is formed with the preceding holding cord.

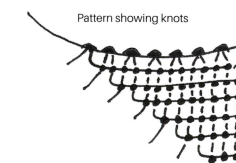

Pattern showing knots

4. Continue in the same way until row 7.

A-5. Row 8: use the holding cord from row 7 to work a horizontal cord from right to left.

6. Rows 9–15: repeat the cords from right to left. Bring together the 2 parts of the leaf by knotting the thread set to one side in the first part on each cord (**A**).

7. When only the holding cord remains, knot this to the choker mount.

8. Repeat all stages for each leaf.

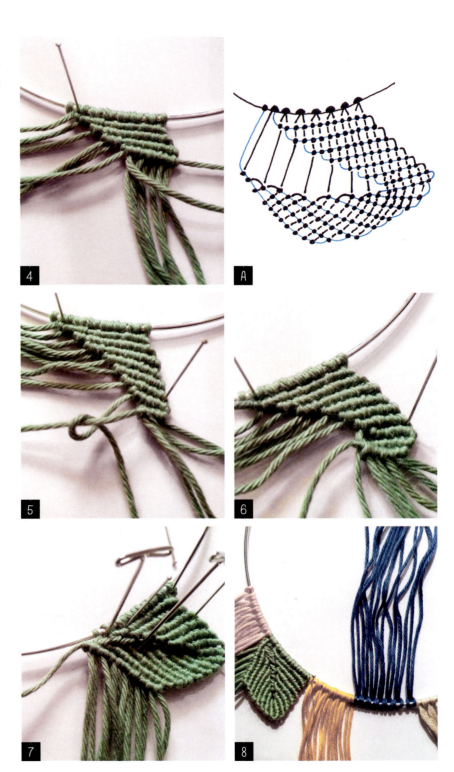

FEATHER BROOCH

A very simple use of half-hitch knots to work cords. In this case the holding cord is a piece of iron wire.

YOU WILL NEED

▸ 8cm (3¼in) galvanised iron wire, 2mm (¹⁄₁₆in) diameter
▸ Two DMC embroidery yarn art. 117 no. 642
▸ 1 glue-on or sew-on brooch mount
▸ Fabric glue
▸ Hot-melt glue gun

STEP BY STEP

1. Cut the yarn into 13cm (5in) lengths. Apply fabric glue to the first 2cm (¾in) of iron wire and wind a length of yarn tightly around it. Wait until it is completely dry.

2-3. Over 5cm (2in), work the yarn 2 by 2 (2 lengths together to give more volume) in the middle of each strand to form a horizontal cord from left to right, using half-hitches (see Technique 6, page 45). 1cm (½in) before the end, apply fabric glue to the iron wire before half-hitch knotting the threads.

4. On the back of the brooch, stick the knots in place along the middle of the strand with the fabric glue. When it is fully dry, stick the feather to the brooch using the glue gun. Trim the threads to form a feather shape. Comb the threads to separate out the strands of the yarn.

SEASHELL NECKLACE

Use circular and 3-D macramé to make the seashell-shaped motifs for this unusual necklace.

YOU WILL NEED

▶ 20m (22yd) ball of linen twine, 1mm (¹⁄₂₅in) diameter
▶ DMC embroidery yarn art. 117 two no. 4030, one no. 4077, one no. 51
▶ 1 silver chain
▶ 6 silver jump rings
▶ Jewellery pliers
▶ Fabric glue

NOTE

The holding cord travels in a spiral around the starting knot. The working threads are set on progressively as you work. The 3-D aspect is created by increasing or decreasing the number of working threads.

Pattern showing knots

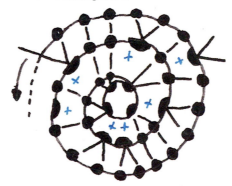

STEP BY STEP

1. Shell no. 1: cut one 60cm (23½in) length of linen twine, sixteen 30cm (11¾in) lengths of embroidery yarn no. 4030 and twelve 20cm (7¾in) lengths of yarn no. 4030. Set on four 30cm (11¾in) lengths of embroidery yarn, folded in half over the linen holding cord. Slip the end of the linen cord through last knot to create a starting loop.

2. Set on lengths at regular intervals to increase the circles: firstly use the 30cm (11¾in) lengths, then the 20cm (7¾in) lengths. Pin each new circle to keep your work flat.

3. When you reach the end of the holding cord, push the centre out from the middle to make it 3-D. Cut the threads off 2cm (¾in) from the last circle and glue them inside using fabric glue.

4. Shell no. 2: cut one 100cm (39½in) linen twine holding cord, twenty 30cm (11¾in) lengths of linen twine, twelve 30cm (11¾in) of embroidery yarn no. 4030. Set the embroidery yarn lengths onto the first circle: (1 length, then 2 lengths onto the second circle on either side of the first, etc).

Shell no. 3: one 100m (109yd) holding cord of linen twine, four 30cm (11¾in) lengths linen twine, twelve 30cm (11¾in) lengths of embroidery yarn no. 4077.

Shell no. 4: one 80cm (31½in) linen twine holding cord, fifteen 20cm (7¾in) lengths of embroidery yarn no. 51. Use the same finishing technique as for shell 1.

TO FINISH

A. Assemble the shells using the jump rings as shown. Open the rings using jewellery pliers and hook them between the knots. Attach the chain at either end.

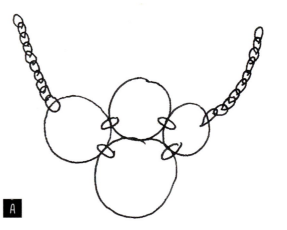

LITTLE PATTERNED BAG

A traditional little macramé bag, highlighted
with Cavandoli embroidery.

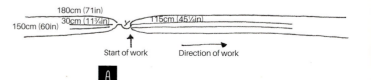

180cm (71in)
30cm (11¾in)
150cm (60in)
115cm (45¼in)

Start of work

Direction of work

YOU WILL NEED

- 60m (66yd) natural cabled cotton twine, 1.5mm (1/16in) diameter
- DMC Woolly Wool col. 081 and 051
- Piece of card 16 x 10cm (6¼ x 4in)
- 1cm (½ in) high card spacer
- Used cotton reels
- Fabric glue
- Crochet hook

Bag size is 17 x 13cm (6¾ x 5in)

STEP BY STEP

SHOULDER STRAP

A. From the cotton twine, cut two 580cm (228in) lengths (working threads) and two 185cm (73in) lengths (leader cords). Wind the lengths onto used cotton reels so you do not get them tangled up. Align the 4 lengths as shown. Set aside 180cm (71in) of the working threads and 30cm (11¾in) of the leader cords (these will be used for the main body of the bag) and tie a temporary overhand knot.

1-2. Tie an initial tight flat knot against the temporary knot (see Technique 3, page 23), then tie a series of flat knots spaced 1cm (½in) apart. To ensure regular spacing, use the 1cm (½in) strip of card spacer. Work an 85cm (33½in) braid of spaced flat knots and then undo the temporary overhand knot.

3. Cut a 100cm (39½in) length of cotton twine (holding cord) and place the length across your knotting board as shown.

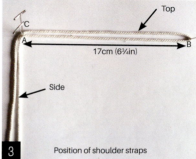

Top

C

A

17cm (6¾in)

B

Side

Position of shoulder straps

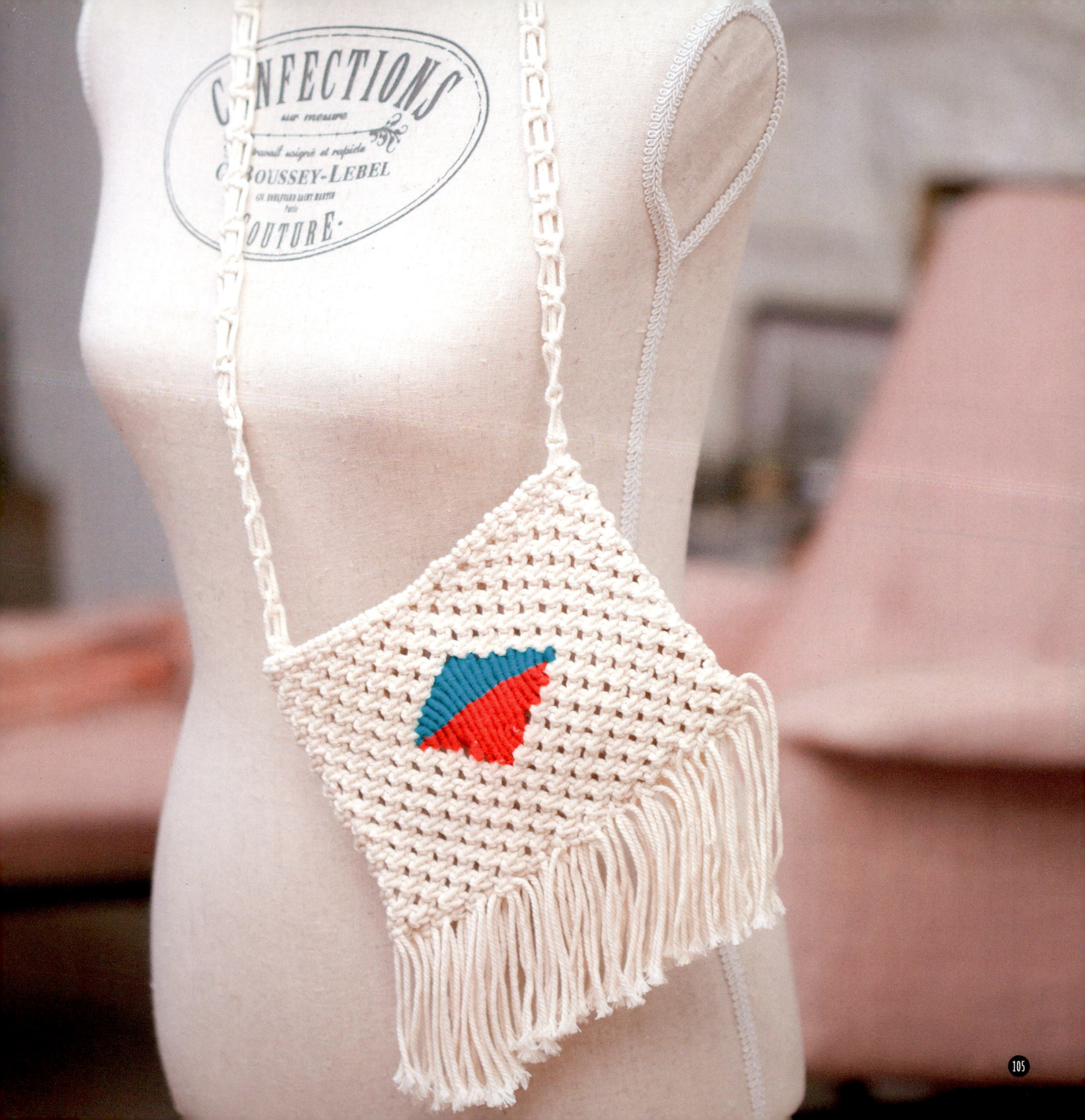
sur mesure
BOUSSEY-LEBEL

4. Cut forty-four 180cm (71in) lengths of cotton twine. Set 22 lengths, folded in 2, loop down, onto the top of the holding cord between A and B (**3**).

5-6. Unpin the holding cord from your knotting board so you can work in a panel. At point B, insert the shoulder strap after one of the knots using another flat knot around the holding cord (the leader cords of the shoulder strap under the holding cord) and the working threads on top).

7. Set on the other 22 lengths between B and C and fold in half.

B and 3. Move the work along and pin it so that the 2 lengths that are still free (points A and C) are facing you. Cut a new 180cm (71in) length, and fold it in half and set on around the 2 lengths in order to close the top of the bag.

8. Slip the shoulder strap threads either side of these 2 new threads.

9. Separate the strands into 2 groups of 4.

10. Tie 1 flat knot with each group of 4.

11. From now on the work is formed in a tube-shape and not as a flat panel. Slip the large piece of cardboard inside the tube so you do not get the threads muddled.

12. Continue row 1 of flat knots around the tube. Alternate the flat knots to create a staggered effect (see Technique 5, page 45). Continue in the same way until row 5.

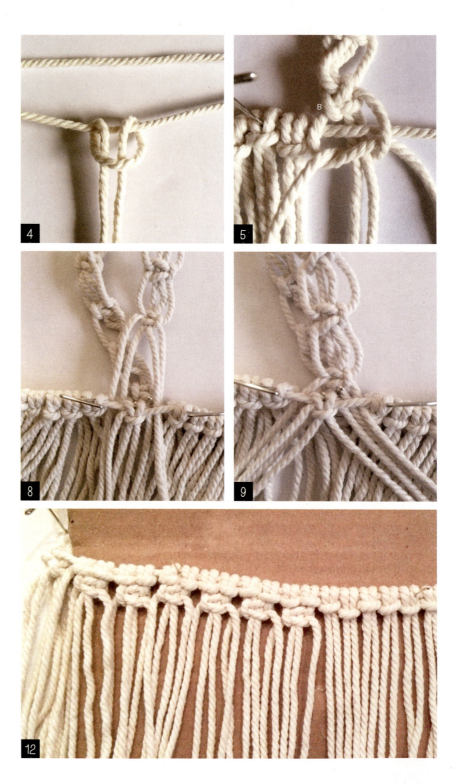

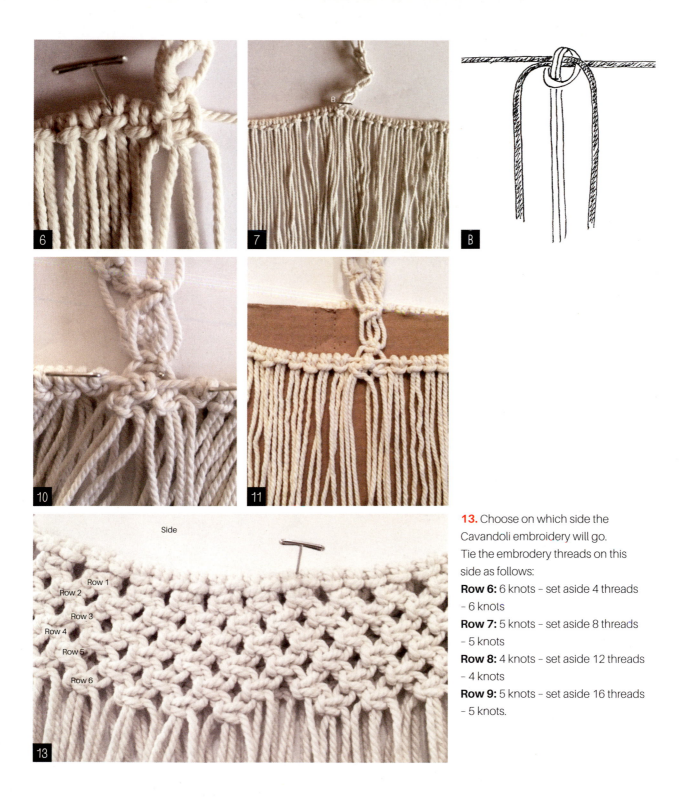

13. Choose on which side the Cavandoli embroidery will go. Tie the embroidery threads on this side as follows:

Row 6: 6 knots – set aside 4 threads – 6 knots

Row 7: 5 knots – set aside 8 threads – 5 knots

Row 8: 4 knots – set aside 12 threads – 4 knots

Row 9: 5 knots – set aside 16 threads – 5 knots.

14. Row 10: continue as for row 8.
Row 11: continue as for row 7.
Row 12: continue as for row 6.
Row 13: continue as for row 5.

15-16. Continue the rows of alternate knots from row 14 to row 18 right around the tube.

17-18. To close the bottom, line up the knots on the two sides of the last row, one against the other. Tie them together with flat knots using the front and back leader cords and the front and back working threads. Trim off the threads to form a 10cm (4in) fringe.

19. For the Cavandoli embroidery, add a 15cm (6in) cotton twine length in the centre of the diamond. Pin it firmly in place. It will be held in place after the cords have been worked.

20. Cut a 50cm (19¾in) length of wool no. 081 and tie vertical cords row by row (see Technique 7, page 86), from left to right, then from right to left on the following row. Use a crochet hook to help you catch hold of the threads at the points of the diamond. When only 10cm (4in) of thread is remaining, tuck it inside and use a new 50cm (19¾in) length. Half way through, change colour and use a 50cm (19¾in) length of wool no. 051.

21. When finished, turn the bag inside out. Use fabric glue to stick down the ends of the wool and then trim to the required length.

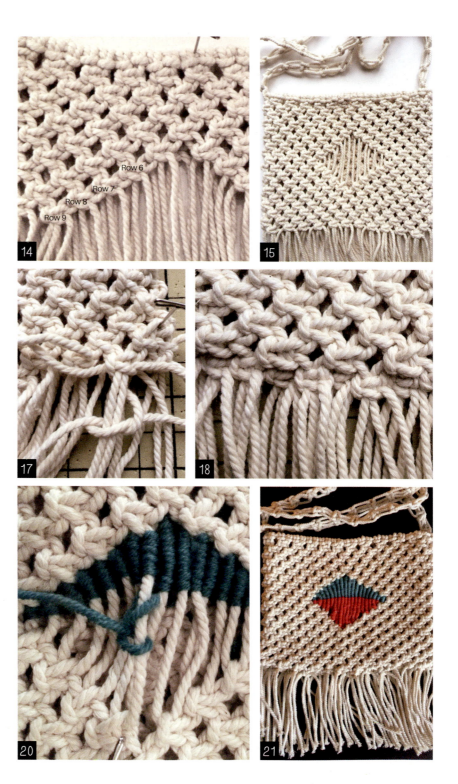

TECHNIQUE 9

ASIAN KNOTS

This is an introduction to decorative knots from China and Japan. They were originally used mostly in dressmaking to make buttons. Worked as braids, these elaborate knots can be used for jewellery. They have a decorative function and can represent forms such as flowers and butterflies, or they can symbolise luck, virtue, the circle of life, etc. They are generally knotted individually but can be joined together with technical knots. There is a huge range of Asian knots, but I have only tackled four here.

JOSEPHINE KNOT

Can be tied using one or several threads in each strand.

PIPA KNOT

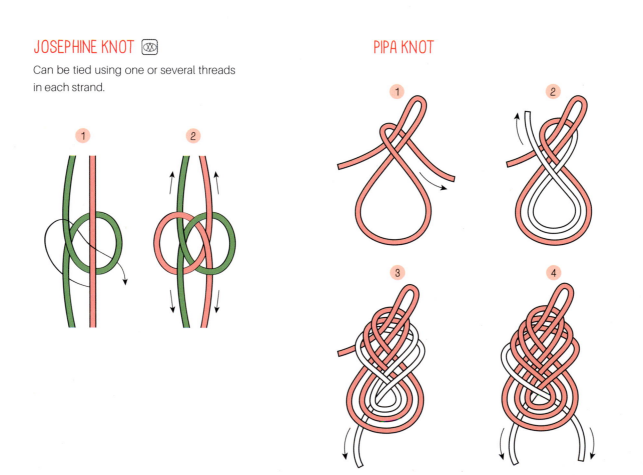

GOOD LUCK KNOT

This knot is made using knots twice tied on top of each other. It is a lucky charm knot. See page 118, steps 2–4.

TIGHT FLAT BUTTON KNOT

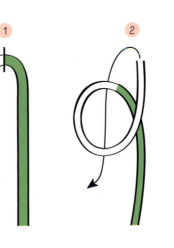

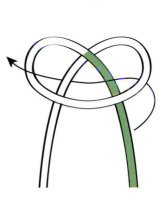

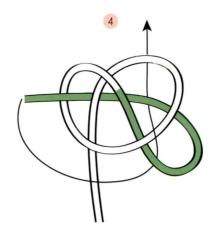

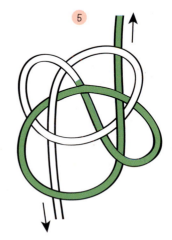

JOSEPHINE BRACELET

Create this colourful bracelet using scoubidou laces and the Josephine knot.

YOU WILL NEED (FOR ONE BRACELET)

▸ 50cm (19¾in) scoubidou laces: 2 blue and 2 yellow
▸ 10mm (⅜in) wide ribbon clamp
▸ Tea light
▸ Jewellery pliers

STEP BY STEP

1. This knot is made with groups of 2 laces in each colour used in parallel. Pin down the 4 laces.

2. Starting 4cm (1½in) down the lace, make an initial loose loop with the 2 left-hand laces.

3. Make another loop with the 2 right-hand laces, passing it under, over and through. Adjust the loops to make them look neat and even and form a 2cm (¾in) wide knot. Pull the laces gently downwards.

4. Make 4 other knots using the different widths shown.

5. Cut the laces off 2cm (¾in) from the first and last knot. Hold the ends of the groups of 2 laces in the tea-light flame to melt them together.

6. Slip the ends of the laces into the clamps and squeeze closed using the jewellery pliers. Put a piece of fabric between the pliers and the clamp so you do not damage the clamp.

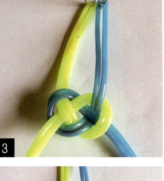

2cm (¾in)

2.5cm (1in)

3cm (1¼in)

2.5cm (1in)

2cm (¾in)

PIPA TWIST CHOKER

This pattern consists of two Pipa knots: one overhand knot with a loop and the other in the form of a ball. It is assembled as a traditional Asian button fastening but used here to make an eye-catching choker.

YOU WILL NEED

▶ 1 ball of lime green wool (not too thick)
▶ 1 silver choker, preferably with a barrel-screw clasp.
▶ A yarn needle with a large eye
▶ 1 manual or mechanical French knitter

STEP BY STEP

1. Using the French knitter, make one 100cm (39½in) length of French knitting using the lime green wool and another of 120cm (47¼), following the instructions that come with the knitter. Ensure that a 20cm (7¾in) length of yarn remains once you have completed the length of French knitting. Finish the lengths.

2. To make the Pipa knot, fold the length of French knitting in two so that the right-hand section is 12cm (4¾in) in length.

3. Form the first loop using the longer length, 10cm (4in) high.

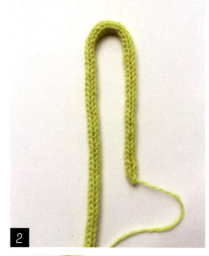

4. The longer length is wrapped around the loop.

5. Repeat 4 times.

6. Pass the length through the last loop. Set to one side.

7. For the Pipa knot with the button, use the 120cm (47¼in) length. Fold in two so that the right-hand section is 20cm (7¼in) in length (see Technique 9, Pipa Knot, page 110 and **C**).

A. Work a tight flat button (see Technique 9, page 111).

B. Pull on each length in turn to draw the flat knot attractively tight. Bring the ends under the knot. Pull tight to give it a rounded shape.

C. Make another Pipa knot.

TO FINISH

8-9. Turn the knots inside out and use the surplus yarn to sew up the two ends through the links of the French knitting. At the same time, sew down the loops to keep them neat and flat. If the lengths of French knitting are too long (it depends how tight you pull them), unravel them a little.

10. Undo the clasp on the choker and slide it through the stitches of the first loops and under the knots in the centre. Centre the knots on the choker.

LUCKY CHARM EARRINGS

An unusual use of good luck knots made with scoubidou laces and decorated with gold-plated wire.

YOU WILL NEED

- ▸ Two 50cm (19¾in) black scoubidou laces
- ▸ Two 50cm (19¾in) lengths of gold-plated wire
- ▸ Two clip-on earring backs
- ▸ Hot-melt glue gun

STEP BY STEP (FOR ONE EARRING)

1. Twist the gold wire around a scoubidou lace. This forms your basic length.

2. Fold in half in the middle. Pin securely to your knotting board. Make the loops. Each loop should be 4.5cm (1¾in) in length.

3-4. Fold the loops one by one clockwise. The top loop turns down towards the strands. Turn the right loop up. Turn the strands up. Turn the left loop right and slip it under the curl created by the top loop to finish the knot. Start another knot in an anticlockwise direction: top, left, bottom and right. Slip the right loop under the curl created by the top loop. Now, the knot is finished. Gently stretch out each loop. Do the same for the second earring.

5. Fold the laces behind and cut off, leaving no more than 1cm (¼in).

6. Stick the earring onto the clip-on using the hot-melt glue gun. Repeat for the second earring.

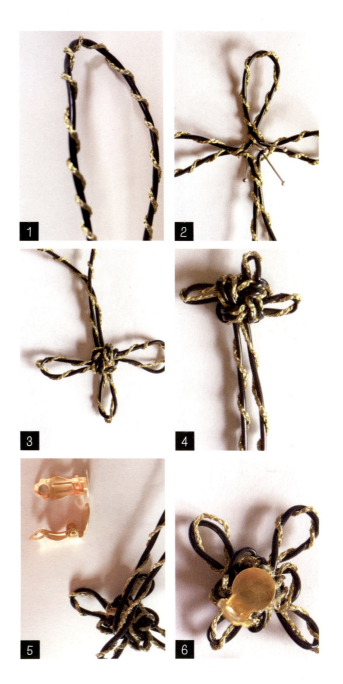

JERSEY NECKLACE

A jersey yarn necklace that looks great over a round-neck top or worn with a strappy top for a cool summer look.

YOU WILL NEED

▸ 25m (27yd) blue Hoooked Zpagetti jersey yarn
▸ Fabric glue

STEP BY STEP

1. Cut three 80cm (31½in) lengths of jersey yarn. 3cm (1¼in) along each length. Tie a collecting knot by wrapping one length around the other 3 (see Technique 1, page 8). Work a tight 3-ply plait (see Technique 2, page 22).

2. Cut twelve 180cm (71in) lengths, and fold them in half. Set the 12 lengths onto the centre of the plait.

3. Divide into 6 groups of 4 threads each.

4. Work a braid of 2 flat knots with each group (see Technique 3, page 23).

5. Turn each braid in on itself to form a pea knot (see Technique 3, page 23).

6. Tie a flat knot to hold the pea knot in place.

7. Add a 40cm (15¾in) leader thread and work a horizontal cord along it (see Technique 6, page 45). Setting aside the first 6 and the last 6 threads, tie 3 rows of alternate knots (see Technique 5, page 45). Divide the strands into groups of 12 threads.

8. Using the first thread as a leader, work a diagonal cord from left towards the bottom right. Using the last thread as a leader, work a diagonal cord from right towards the bottom left.

9. Repeat this over 5 rows. At the 6th row, set aside the first 8 and last 8 threads. With the threads you have set aside, work a vertical cord on each side (see Technique 7, page 86).

10. Tie a flat knot to link the last two cords. Glue the ends of the leader cords firmly into place on the back of the work with fabric glue. Trim off the threads to 7cm (2¾in).

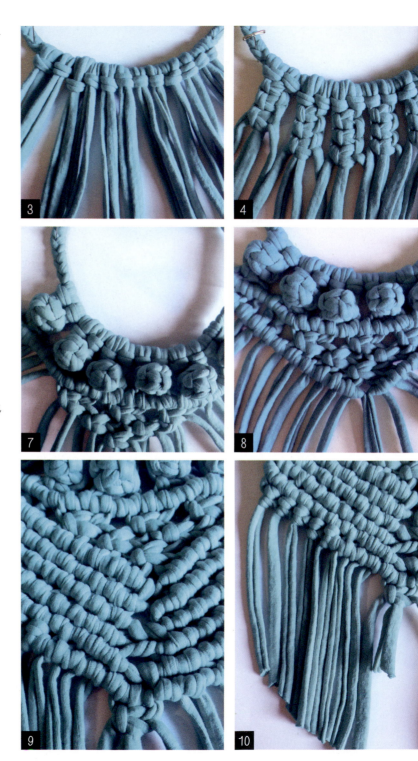

VEST TOP BACK PANEL

Customise a vest top for a really summery look that is all your own.

YOU WILL NEED

- 1 vest top
- 12m (13yd) of DMC Hooooked Zpagetti jersey yarn art. 800 in grey or a colour of your choice
- Fabric glue

STEP BY STEP

1. Cut three 170cm (67in) lengths of yarn. Fold them in half. Cut two 20cm (7¾in) holding cords, one for each strap.

2. Set 3 strands onto each holding cord, loop upwards. Leaving a 3cm (1¼in) gap, add a new 20cm (7¾in) holding cord. Tie a horizontal cord, then a series of alternating flat knots using a single leader cord (see Technique 5, page 45). Repeat the stages given above for the other strap.

3. This is one complete strap.

A, B. Where the two straps meet (point C), form a loop with the two strands as show in **5**. Pin.

4-5. Cut a 50cm (19¼in) length of yarn, and fold it in half. Put the length into place, positioning the loop in the middle of the other two. Pin.

6. Attach it all using a flat knot. Adjust the whole thing as necessary and then pull tight.

7. Using the 4 strands from the flat knot, work another flat knot. Work two 3-ply flat knots on either side

8. Cut a 30cm (11¾in) leader cord. Work a horizontal cord using all the strands.

9. Work 2 diagonal cords using the first and last strands of the previous cord as leader cords. Add a last 20cm (7¾in) leader cord. Work a horizontal cord. At this stage, 2 of the strands can no longer be used as they are too short and so they should be threaded through to the back of the work.

10. Thread the leader cord through to the back and secure in place using fabric glue. Place the work on the vest top so you can see where you need to cut off the top's existing straps. Trim off the strands 2cm (¾in) underneath the last cord. Stitch them in place on the inside of the vest top. Sew together along the cords.

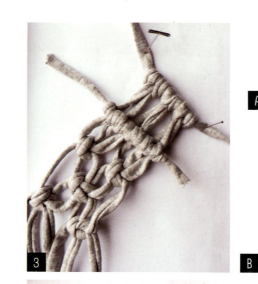

3

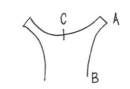

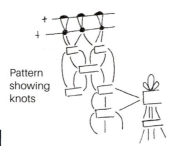

A

B

Pattern showing knots

6

7

9

10

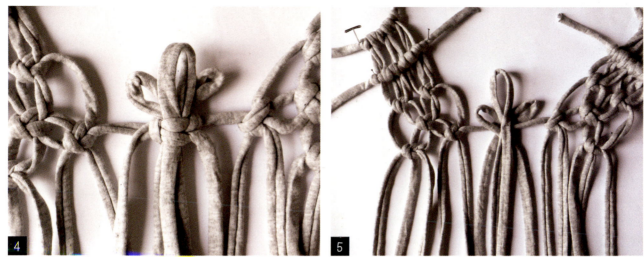

THANKS

I would like to thank Laurence W. for having thought of me, Adeline L. for the trust she showed in me and everyone who has participated in the making of this book. Big thanks to the men in my life who have been very patient. This book is dedicated to my parents, for their unwavering support.

First published in Great Britain in 2016
by Search Press Limited, Wellwood,
North Farm Road, Tunbridge Wells, Kent TN2 3DR

Original title: Macramé Pas à Pas

Copyright © 2015 by Éditions Marie Claire – Société d'Information et de Créations – SIC

English translation by Burravoe Translation Services

Director of publishing: Thierry Lamarre
Project Editor: Adeline Lobut
Design and production: Claire Rougerie
Photographs: Emmanuela Cino
Styling: Karine Villame
Editing/proofreading: Noëlie Favreau
Graphic design and lay-out: Either studio

ISBN: 978-1-78221-356-7

The Publishers and author can accept no responsibility for any consequences arising from the information, advice or instructions given in this publication.

Readers are permitted to reproduce any of the items in this book for their personal use, or for the purposes of selling for charity, free of charge and without the prior permission of the Publishers. Any use of the items for commercial purposes is not permitted without the prior permission of the Publishers.

Printed in China